TAKE THIS DISH and TWIST IT

by GEORGE DURAN

MEREDITH® BOOKS / DES MOINES, IOWA

Meredith® Books
1716 Locust Street
Des Moines, Iowa 50309–3023
meredithbooks.com
Printed in the United States of America.

First Edition.
Library of Congress Control Number: 2008924203
ISBN: 978-0-696-23943-4

Photos of George by Pam Francis
Food photos by Blaine Moats and Scott Little
Illustrations on pages 14–15 by Eileen Stevens

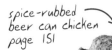
spice-rubbed beer can chicken page 151

WITHDRAWN

CONTENTS

From breakfast to dessert and everything in between, you're going to love eating your way through this book. You can thank me later.

215
Ice Cream Club Sandwich

202 Cinnamon-Banana Milk Shake

59
Layered Caprese Salad

31
Sun-Dried Tomato Cheddar Grits

microwave chicken curry page 125

OEOICATION

To **ZOVIG GULDALIAN,** my MOTHER, for showing me, my brother Raffi,
and my sister Talar, how much you love us by overfeeding us
your magnificent Armenian meals throughout our childhood.

ACKNOWLEOGMENTS

DAVID DOMEDION, culinary producer.
Don't let his humble look fool you;
this guy is brilliant, masterful, and
meticulous in the kitchen.

PETER SHERMAN, writer extraordinaire.
Did you actually think that with
my short attention span I could
properly structure my thoughts
without this genius?

These are my real-life guinea pigs, **MY DEAR FRIENDS,** who courageously
taste-tested each of my recipes and objectively rated each dish.
Did I mention they all washed my dishes at one point or another?

EILEEN   KELVYN   WALTER   MARK   AOLAI   PAUL+VIV   YOSARA   AMANOA

Last but not least I want to thank all of the people that have made an impact on my career and the making
of this book. Thanks to the entire staff at Stone House Productions, including John, Cheryl, and Craig ... for
believing in me, to the Food Network for taking a chance on a bold idea, and my best friends Armand and Vache
for the wild adventures we endured. Thank you, Tim Bright, for the best music composer the Food Network's ever
had. My French entourage, Tanya, Thomas, Didar, Julien, David (POS #1), Jackie (POS #2), Nick (POS #3),
Joseph, Ludo, and Carla . . . for making my three years in Paris the most memorable ever, merci. Lisa and Eric,
for making this book happen. To the entire staff at Meredith including, Erin Burns, Jessica Saari, Stephanie
Karpinske, Pam Francis, Gregory Kayko, Amy Nichols, Jan Miller, Mick Schnepf, Jennifer Darling, and
everyone else. Thanks to the folks at Calphalon, Weber Grills, Progressive International, and Oxo. Finally, to
all of my loving and faithful fans from *Ham on the Street* . . . just so you know, the best is yet to come! GD

WELCOME TO MY WORLD
That's right, I'm talking to you.

Did you know that you're living in the midst of a culinary revolution that has turned the bland, unimaginative menus of the past into an explosion of fresh, flavorful meals? And you're happy to dig into the revolutionary results—as long as someone else is doing the cooking.

Pots and pans? Great for heating up canned soup! Ovens? Perfect place to store pots and pans! Refrigerators? Exclusive home to beer, soda, and that bottle of (three-year-old) Thousand Island dressing! Okay, perhaps that Thousand Island is two years old—but the end result is the same: You've been steering clear of the kitchen.

But those days are over. Because you wouldn't be reading this if you didn't have at least a little interest in unleashing your inner gastronome. And that's why I wrote this book. To lure you into your kitchen and keep you there—by any means necessary.

Settle down, I come in peace. And better yet—I brought Twinkies! Not to mention burgers, banana splits, hot dogs, pizza, pancakes, casseroles, fried chicken, frittatas—and more! Obviously, we're not talking "health food" here. But we are talking fresh, flavorful food. You'll find recipes that use familiar comfort-food ingredients to create simple, refined dishes. And that is healthy. Because the first step toward eating well is knowing exactly what it is you're eating. And the best way to do *that* is to do the cooking yourself.

Of course, I realize that just giving you recipes is not enough. In this information age, your hyperstimulated brain demands more. So this cookbook was conceived not only to capture your short attention span with tantalizing recipes but to keep it with an entertaining array of tips, tidbits, factoids, gadgets, musings, and various other monkeyshines. You can pick out appetizers for your next big party, check out what to do if a kitchen disaster strikes, or just play a quick game of "What'd I Fry?"

Whatever page you land on, I hope this book inspires you to bring people to your table. A table where there's plenty of laughter as you see how enjoyable, entertaining, and easy it can be to prepare and enjoy the foods that make us feel so good.

Bon Appétit!

George Duran

DURAN

YO

KITC

CULINARY SCHOOL?
SAVE YOUR DOUGH
(TO BUY MORE FOOD!) BECAUSE I HAVE
A WHOLE PANTRYLOAD OF TIPS, TRIVIA,
AND KNOW-HOW THAT WILL TAKE YOUR
GASTRONOMIC GAME TO THE NEXT
DELECTABLE LEVEL.

DURANCTIONARY: (n. durr-ANN-shun-airy)
a guide to oddball culinary terms compiled by some guy named George Duran

Sacré bleu! America's culinary vocabulary is overflowing with so many international entries, it can make your head spin! Well, get ready to have it spin in the other direction, because I have a few contributions of my own. You may be familiar with the terms in purple—but read the ones in red and you'll sink your teeth into a bit of Duran-style culinary terms!

À LA MODE: served with a scoop of ice cream on top, such as apple pie à la mode

À LA LOAD: topping any food (I mean ANY food— think pizza!) with multiple scoops of ice cream

. . . .

AL DENTE: cooked to be firm when bitten, not too soft; usually pertains to pasta

MAL DENTE: when you forget your pasta is cooking and return to a pile of durum wheat mush

. . . .

BOYSENBERRY: a cross of a blackberry, loganberry, and raspberry developed by Rudolph Boysen in 1923

BOYS 'N' BERRIES: the new musical I'm writing about the rise to power of the Smucker family (desperately in need of financing—Anyone? Anyone? Mom?)

. . . .

BROCCOLINI: a hybrid of broccoli and Chinese broccoli; has thin stems that are like asparagus in both texture and flavor

BROCCOTINI: my brief, ill-fated attempt to create a healthy cocktail (never again)

. . . .

CHIFFONADE: a mixture of fine, ribbon-cut vegetables and/or herbs used in salads, soups, etc.

CHIFFON-ODD: taking the only herbs and spices you have in the house, mixing them all together, and hoping for the best!

DEMI-SEC: a French expression that means half dry, which is used to describe sweet Champagnes with up to 5 percent sugar

DEMI-SICK: the unpleasant period of time between that pleasant Champagne buzz and the thundering morning-after hangover

. . . .

DURIAN: the edible fruit of the tree *Durio zibethinus*; has a hard, thorn-covered rind, pulpy flesh, and an odor some find pleasant but most find nauseating; grown and widely revered in Southeast Asia, where it is known as the "King of Fruits": not generally available fresh in the United States; however, preserved dried durian can be found in Asian markets.

GEORGE DURIAN: my given name, which I had to change when I became a chef because the crowds of screaming fans in Asia were making my life a living hell—and the crowds of disgusted fans everywhere else were making my life a living hell!

. . . .

FLAMBÉ: any food served in flaming liquor such as brandy

BOMBÉ: when you skip the whole "flaming" part and just drink the brandy with your steak

. . . .

FOIE GRAS: the liver of a goose or duck that has been specially fattened for use as a culinary delicacy

SPA GRAS: a fantasy spa treatment where your entire body is submerged in a vat of warm butter (at least it's *my* fantasy)

FRAPPÉ: a frozen, mushy mixture of fruit juices served as a dessert or appetizer

RAPPÉ: a hot mix of flava, funk, and soul served out on a bling-bling platter

GOURMAND: a person who loves good food, often to excess

GOURMANDIBLE: the jaw of a gourmand, which is actually ten times stronger than the average jaw

JULEP: a sweet, syrupy drink that was traditionally given with medicine

BREW-LEP: a mug of ice-cold beer; sure to cure what ails ya!

MAÎTRE D': the person in charge of the day-to-day operation of a restaurant, including food-preparation quality, service, and guest seating

MAÎTRE F': the person responsible for the day-to-day screw-ups in the restaurant, including the mishandling of food preparation, presentation, and especially service

OENOPHILE: one who exhibits a disciplined devotion to, and affection for, wine

FRYOPHILE: one (like me) who loves, seeks out, and must experience the maximum number of different types of fried food

PESCETARIAN: a vegetarian who eats fish; also known as a pescevegetarian

PERPLEXITARIAN: a vegetarian who will eat beef, chicken, veal, ostrich, reindeer, and crocodiles— but not fish

PLONK: British slang for inferior, cheap wine

DRONK: what you get when you drink too much plonk

SAUCIER: a cook or chef whose specialty is the preparation of sauces

WAFFLEIER: a chef, cook, relative, friend, or roommate who specializes in the preparation of waffles

SHABU-SHABU: a Japanese dish where thinly sliced meats and vegetables are boiled quickly in broth, then served with an assortment of sauces for dipping

CRABU-CRABU: substitute imitation crab for the thinly sliced meat; a delicacy in Norway (Well, once I introduce it to them it will be, you can take that to the bank!)

SOMMELIER: a trained, educated wine professional, commonly found in fine restaurants, who specializes in every aspect of wine service

DUMBELLIER: any sommelier who talks you into buying an overpriced bottle of crappy wine

TURKISH DELIGHT: popular candy in the Middle East; known for its rubbery texture; made by mixing cornstarch or gelatin with sugar, honey, and fruit juice or jelly; often colored green or pink, cut into squares, and coated with powdered sugar

AMERICAN DELIGHT: a Twinkie

GEORGE'S TOP 10 MUST-HAVE INGREDIENTS

I love New York, but living in the big city is not without its inherent dangers.

For instance, when a group of ravenous friends arrive at my apartment after a night out on the town, they expect their "old pal the chef" to offer them gourmet sustenance. That's why I *always* keep my favorite ingredients on hand. These, my friends, are items I cannot (and *will* not) live without.

1. CURRY PASTE. Oh, my dear, sweet (well, not sweet actually, but you get my meaning) curry paste! Your cousin, the powder, is great and all, but you offer such a distinct, pungent aroma. It's one that can take even the most mundane sauce to the next level. You are my number one must-have ingredient.

2. NONSTICK COOKING SPRAY. Possibly the most underrated invention in the history of food. I love this stuff so much, I bought the company! Okay, that's a lie—but I *do* buy it by the case. How did I ever live without it? I *didn't*.

3. BACON. Every Sunday I go to my kitchen, kneel toward my fridge, and pray to the bacon gods. It's a ritual that was born the day I had my first bite of this mouthwatering delight. And it's not just the taste, of course. It's the aroma. There's nothing more comforting to me (and possibly annoying to my neighbors) than filling my apartment with the smell of those sizzling strips of heaven. My absolute favorite brand is by Father's Country Hams in Ohio. But then again, I haven't tasted every brand out there—yet!

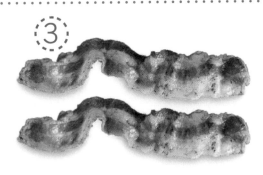

4. GROUND CUMIN. This spice complements the natural sweetness of many dishes but also adds some earthiness to spicier recipes. It's also a fantastic "mystery spice" to add to unexpected recipes—because nothing beats playing with your guests' minds as they wonder just what that unusual addition is.

5. COCONUT MILK. The unsweetened variety is always stocked in my pantry. The stuff lasts for months and can replace heavy cream in a flash. It also makes for a luxurious, tropical bath! (Or so I'm told by some friends from the tropics.)

6. RED WINE. That's right, the grape is not *just* for drinking (though it really is quite good when drunk!). Write this down: For any recipe that calls for any type of liquid, you can replace that liquid with red wine. The rule of thumb for choosing the right wine to cook with is simple: Cook with the wine you are drinking! You'll never go wrong—until you run out, of course!

7. CHIPOTLE HOT SAUCE. Of the thousands of hot pepper sauces available, this is the one my taste buds crave. Why? Because it doesn't burn them beyond recognition, that's why! Chipotle hot sauce has just the right amount of spice, plus a rich, vinegary smokiness that goes with everything, including desserts (check out my Hot and Spicy Brownies)! Tabasco makes a good one, but feel free to search online for many, *many* others.

8. PINE NUTS. I love pine trees. Not because of that fresh, foresty scent or because they remind me of the holiday season or even for their selfless sacrifice to my futon frame. No, I love pine trees because the nut their cones bear is my all-time favorite. Nothing beats the taste of toasted pine nuts on salads, veggie dishes, and even desserts. And by simply storing them in the freezer, I'm assured there will be pine nuts at my disposal year-round.

9. FRESH CILANTRO. I keep cilantro in my fridge all year long because salsa, guacamole, tacos, and even salads just aren't the same without it. Extend the life of this herb by wrapping the bottom ends with a moist paper towel and placing it in a resealable plastic bag. Blow some CO_2 (aka your breath) into the bag and watch your cilantro stay green and happy for days and days.

10. VANILLA ICE CREAM. I'm not saying vanilla is my favorite flavor. (That honor goes to strawberry ice cream with balsamic vinegar. No lie!) But I can tell you that when your brownies are a tad too dry, when there's just too much chocolate in the cake, or when you want to bring up the flavor of that pie, a scoop (or three) of the sweet, creamy simplicity of vanilla ice cream has a miraculous way of making those problems (and more) disappear.

A FEW OF MY FAVORITE THINGS
Gadgets are an integral part of my kitchen.

My personal collection is an ever-expanding pile of thingamajigs, doohickeys, whatchamacallits, and other indispensable (okay, sometimes useless) contraptions that help make cooking not just easier, but more fun! Here's my top ten list for must-have kitchen tools.

1. SALAD SPINNER. Think I'm just gonna hand dry each leaf of lettuce? Or shake the water from my freshly washed herbs? No way! Forget it! A good salad spinner makes my other gadgets green with envy. And this one is my absolute all-time favorite.

2. INSTANT ONION CHOPPER. When you need that onion quickly chopped without shedding a single, solitary tear, this device is a timesaver extraordinaire. There are many varieties out there, but as far as I'm concerned, this one is all you'll ever need.

3. OIL THERMOMETER. I learned the hard way that an oil thermometer is essential to deep-frying. And deep-frying is an essential part of my job (and life!). So take it from me, knowing the exact temperature of the oil you're about to drop that Snickers bar in is always smart.

4. GARLIC PRESS. There are few things more disconcerting than biting into a big, uncooked hunk of garlic in your stew. So a garlic press is an absolute necessity for the dispersal of that most indispensable of ingredients.

5. PICKLE PICKER. It's not just that I love to say "pickle picker" out loud (really, it isn't!). It's also that this thing actually makes it fun to pick everything from pickles to olives—even eggshells!

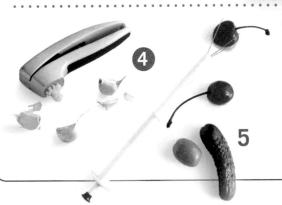

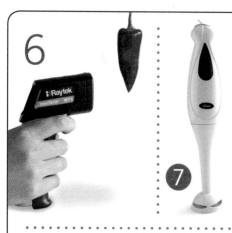

6. LASER TEMPERATURE GUN GAUGE.
This was a gift from my buddy Armand, and even though he's not a cook, he thought I would love it. I do! Any time I need to know what temperature a pan is before I sear, I pull this baby out and point and shoot. It's also great for checking out the temperature of every surface in my apartment. Hours of enjoyment!

7. HAND BLENDER.
When things go wrong in the kitchen, I can always rely on my hand blender to step in and save the day. It's a fairly cheap gadget that really comes in handy when you're making soups and sauces. If you need to buy one thing on this list, this is it. But make sure to buy the one that has all of the other cool attachments!

8. FOOD PROCESSOR WITH ATTACHMENTS.
It's not really the processor that I love so much. It's more about the two standard attachments that come with it. One instantly grates anything and everything (cheese, cabbage, carrots, etc.), while the other makes instant sliced chips out of any chippable thing you can think of (potatoes, turnips, parsnips, etc.).

9. DOUGH SCRAPER.
This gets my vote for the gadget most people don't have but that they absolutely should! I'd marry mine if I could, I love it so much! Why the devotion? Because nothing aggravates me more than trying to scrape chopped ingredients from a cutting board to the bowl. This baby does it with one quick, efficient swoop.

10. MY IPOD.
Okay, so this isn't technically a culinary gadget, but my kitchen simply couldn't function without it. Whether I'm chopping to the beat of some crunk, flambéing to a little flamenco, roasting to classic rock, or sauteing to ska—music adds inspiration to even the most mundane moments in my kitchen.

MASTER YOUR DISASTER:

It's a fear that leaves many a chef quaking in his or her clogs. I speak, of course, of the dreaded Kitchen Catastrophe!

But guess what? You have *nothing* to fear. Just do me one favor: *Don't panic!* Take a look at some of these disaster scenarios and remember, there is no such thing as a mistake in the kitchen—only big opportunities for a little ingenuity.

PROBLEM: I put way too much salt in my soup. Now what do I do?

SOLUTION: Put that can opener away! Oversalting soup is one of the most common problems that the homemade-soup maker will confront. First take a look in the mirror (or, if one isn't handy, your shiniest spoon) and acknowledge that you, sir or madam, are the problem. You violated chef rule number one: Always taste as you go. Season little by little and always taste, taste, taste, taste! But since you ignored that rule, here's what to do: Peel a large potato, cut it in half, and add it to the soup. Simmer until the potato is cooked, then discard it, and taste your newly not oversalted soup! That nifty potato absorbs extra salt like magic. No potato handy? Add more liquid to the soup to thin it out.

PROBLEM: I threw some burgers on the grill, then went inside to grab a cold drink. When I came back, the burgers were charred beyond recognition on the outside but still not done on the inside. Help!

SOLUTION: I'm no expert (oh wait, I am), but I'm going to guess that your grill heat was just a tad too high. Take those charred burgers, trim off some of the burnt area of the meat, and, if needed, wrap the burgers in some foil. Let them cook slowly on the grill until the inside is done to your liking. A brush of some sweet barbecue sauce or honey right before serving will help mask any residual burnt flavor too!

PROBLEM: I added too much hot sauce to my casserole. Is it ruined?

SOLUTION: I've made this mistake a few times myself, and while I have occasionally attempted to grit my teeth and test the limits of human suffering, the humane thing to do is to simply add some cream to it or serve it with some yogurt on the side.

PROBLEM: I've overcooked my veggies and now they are dull and tasteless.

SOLUTION: Invite all your British friends over and tell them you've got some of "mum's home cookin'"! Aw, just kidding, Brits! Overcooked veggies are all too common here in the colonies too—but they don't have to be tasteless. As long as you have the right ingredients and proper tools, even the most devastated veggies can be salvaged. Simply place them in the food processor and pulse with cream cheese, sour cream, and/or hard-cooked eggs. Season properly with herbs and hot sauce and you have an awesome spread or dip to add life to crackers or raw veggies. (I know you can't screw those up! Just don't cut off your fingers.)

PROBLEM: My sauce and/or gravy is all lumpy!

SOLUTION: You know that fine sieve that's been sitting in the bottom of your gadget drawer ever since your cousin regifted it to you three birthdays ago? Pull it out, dust it off, and pass that gravy through it. Watch those lumps disappear faster than PhotoShop zaps acne. If you're one of the many non-sieve owners out there—don't despair. Just crank up the hand blender and you'll have smooth sauce in no time (well, a little time, but in the grand scheme of life, basically none).

PROBLEM: My friends love chicken but whenever I try to make it for a dinner party, it comes out so dry. The same thing happens with pork. How can I fix that?

SOLUTION: There are few things worse for a host than watching your guests chew endlessly on a leathery piece of meat you made them. Luckily there are ways to inject a little moisture back into your overcooked creation before you foist it on your friends. If you need to serve your meat whole (such as a pork chop), drizzle some extra virgin olive oil on it right before serving. If you are flexible with the meat, shred it with a fork and knife and add chicken stock or any sauce (such as barbecue) to make a nice pulled-chicken wrap. Or just serve the shredded meat alongside some rice.

PROBLEM: I can't peel my hard-cooked eggs!

SOLUTION: Peeling a hard-cooked egg can be as much fun as licking lead paint chips off your living room floor. Okay, slight exaggeration. But the frustration of peeling an egg, microscopic shell fragment by microscopic shell fragment, is one of life's underrated irritants. Resist the urge to fling the thing across the room—instead submerge the egg in a pot of cold water. Then crack it and watch as the water seeps into the cracks. Peeling then gets a little easier, allowing you to get a hold of the membrane under the shell. Peeling under running water also works.

PROBLEM: My brownies, cakes, and other baked goods often turn out burnt but also undercooked.

SOLUTION: Hey, don't be so hard on yourself. It's easy to not follow directions properly. Hold on—no, actually it isn't. But for some reason you thought 350°F meant 500°F! Thankfully there is a simple solution to your problem. First and foremost—do not serve the burnt part. Instead collect the doughy section of the pie, cookie, or cake and serve it with some premium ice cream . . . instant topping!

WHAT'D I FRY?

As the famous final lyric of our national anthem so eloquently states, America is "the land of the free and the home of the brave."

And I for one feel there is no purer way to express this than by exercising one of our most treasured, fundamental freedoms: To deep-fry anything and everything we choose. And then be brave enough to eat it! One fun way to do this? Why, a spirited game of "What'd I Fry?" of course! It's a simple, delicious method for mixing a little mystery into your next party. All you need is a bowl of batter, a bunch of sticks, and plenty of imagination! To get the party started, I've taken a batch of my cornmeal batter and thrown open my fridge for an anything-goes excursion into the boiling oil. All you've got to do is try to guess the tasty treats that are blanketed beneath the corny crust.
The answers are on page 18.

ANSWERS:

Yes, my friends, you *can* fry all of these unusual items. The question is—*should* you? Let your taste buds be the judge of that.

Before you turn up your nose at fried strawberries, eggs, broccoli, and yes, even a pear—you must try it yourself. Make it party. Invite your friends over and fry up anything and everything you've got hanging around in refrigerator. (Note: If something is wearing mold, frying won't help it.)

CORNMEAL BATTER

1	cup cornmeal
⅔	cup corn flour
1	tablespoon sugar
1	teaspoon salt
1	teaspoon baking powder
2	eggs
1½	cups selzer water or club soda
	Oil
	Hot dogs or other foods for frying

1* In a large bowl whisk together the cornmeal, flour, sugar, salt, and baking powder. Add the eggs and half the seltzer and whisk well to combine. Add more seltzer as needed until the batter is thick and the consistency of pancake batter.

2* Heat the oil in a deep-fat fryer to 375°F. Dip the hot dogs (or other foods) in the batter and carefully place them in the hot oil. Fry a few at a time, turning them over from time to time, until they are golden brown, about 2 to 3 minutes total. Drain on paper towels. Serve while still warm.

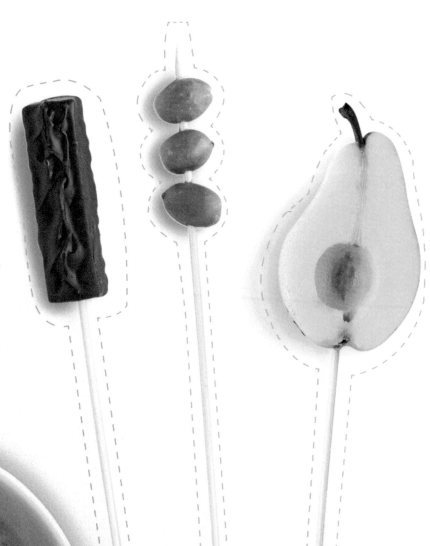

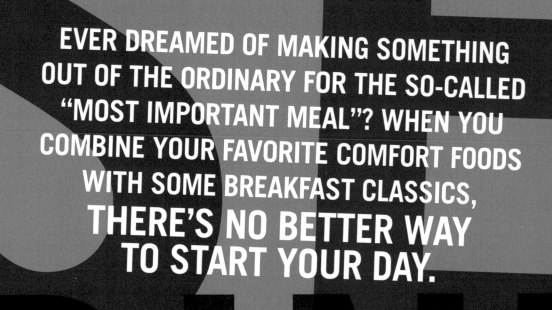

EVER DREAMED OF MAKING SOMETHING OUT OF THE ORDINARY FOR THE SO-CALLED "MOST IMPORTANT MEAL"? WHEN YOU COMBINE YOUR FAVORITE COMFORT FOODS WITH SOME BREAKFAST CLASSICS, **THERE'S NO BETTER WAY TO START YOUR DAY.**

POTATO CHIP SURPRISE

Each day, I look forward to rolling out of bed at the crack of noon to indulge in an overstuffed omelet or syrup-soaked Belgian waffle. **That's right—noon. Because to me, breakfast is a state of mind, not a time of day.**

Of course, I will make exceptions. When I was in culinary school in Paris, a close friend of mine got married. After the reception I was one of the select few invited to spend the weekend at a house her family had rented in the French countryside. Being the selfless, devoted friend that I am (who becomes perhaps a little too selfless and devoted after an evening spent sipping top-shelf Champagne), I offered to whip up a sumptuous, scrumptious breakfast for everyone the following morning. That meant dragging my sleep-deprived, Champagne-soaked self out of bed way too early to head into the local village for supplies. And discovering that, thanks to an obscure French holiday I'd never heard of, not one shop was open!

After taking a moment to remind myself that this is why I never get up early, I scoured the kitchen only to find onions, a few jars of spices, and several bags of potato chips. As nightmare images of me serving my infamous Spicy Potato Chip and Onion Granola filled my head, I was relieved when I looked out the window and saw an herb garden (which provided—not surprising—herbs!) and the house next door (home to an equally early-rising farmer, who graciously gifted me with a dozen eggs).

What do all those ingredients add up to? My now-famous Potato Chip Spanish Tortilla (check out the recipe on page 29), that's what! I marinated the potato chips in the eggs, herbs, and spices, slowly fried the mixture with the onion, finished everything in the oven—and served it. It was a hit! And they all commented on how impressed they were with the "paper-thin potatoes" I'd meticulously sliced. I just nodded, smiled, and went back to bed. Breakfast accomplished!

SPINACH BREAKFAST PIZZA

PREP: 15 minutes / COOK: 15 minutes / BAKE: 9 minutes / YIELD: 4 to 6 servings

I love surprising my friends when I pull this pizza out of the oven for brunch. If you're spinach-phobic, replace it with pretty much any veggie or meat topping. Don't you just love limitless options?

1	(10-ounce) prepared thin pizza crust (such as Boboli)
1	teaspoon extra virgin olive oil
1	(10-ounce) package frozen chopped spinach
8	eggs
	Kosher salt or table salt and freshly ground black pepper
2	tablespoons extra virgin olive oil
1	large onion, chopped (1 cup)
½	cup shredded cheddar cheese (2 ounces)

1* Preheat the oven to 450°F. Brush top of the pizza crust with the 1 teaspoon oil. Place crust directly on the middle rack of the oven; bake for 8 to 10 minutes.

2* While the crust is baking, cook the spinach according to the package directions. Drain, reserving 1 tablespoon of the liquid. Squeeze spinach dry. In a bowl whisk together the eggs and the reserved spinach liquid. Season with salt and pepper. In a 10-inch skillet heat the 2 tablespoons oil over medium heat. Add the onion; cook about 4 minutes or until translucent. Add the spinach, breaking up the pieces, and heat through. Stir the spinach mixture into the eggs and mix well. Lower the heat to low. Pour the egg mixture into the skillet. Cook and gently stir the eggs for 3 to 4 minutes or until they are just set but still moist.

3* Spread the egg mixture evenly over the baked pizza crust and top with the cheese. Bake about 1 minute more or until the cheese is melted and lightly browned. Serve hot.

MYSTERY THINGAMAJIGS ∨

For your next brunch, take this recipe to the next level: Cook it in one of these rotating tabletop pizza makers!

JALAPEÑO CORN CUFFINS

PREP: 15 minutes / BAKE: 20 minutes / YIELD: 12 muffins

These babies may look like cupcakes, but every scrumptiously spicy bite screams muffin! Meet the one-of-a-kind "cuffin."

1½ cups cornmeal
1   cup all-purpose flour
2   tablespoons sugar
2½ teaspoons baking powder
½   teaspoon salt
2   eggs
¾   cup milk
1   (4-ounce) can chopped jalapeño
       chile peppers, drained
¼   cup butter (½ stick), melted
2   (12-ounce) containers
       whipped cream cheese
       Finely chopped red, orange,
         and yellow sweet peppers
       Snipped fresh cilantro (optional)

1 * Preheat the oven to 350°F. Line twelve 2½-inch muffin cups with paper bake cups.

2 * In a large bowl stir together the cornmeal, flour, sugar, baking powder, and salt. In another bowl beat the eggs. Add the milk, jalapeños, and melted butter to the eggs and stir well. Pour the egg mixture into the cornmeal mixture; stir until just combined. (Or use corn muffin mix and add the drained jalapeños to the batter.)

3 * Divide the batter evenly among the muffin cups. Bake for 20 minutes or until lightly browned. Cool completely.

4 * Frost the cuffins with whipped cream cheese, as you would a cupcake, and garnish with the chopped sweet peppers. If desired, sprinkle with snipped cilantro.

GEORGE'S SECRET ∨

Express your artistic excellence by using a pastry bag and different tips to frost your corn cuffins.

CHEESEBURGER FRITTATA

PREP: 10 minutes / COOK: 15 minutes / BROIL: 3 minutes / YIELD: 4 servings

Frittatas offer the creative breakfast chef a delectably blank canvas.
This one in particular is the perfect way to feed your hamburger-
loving friends at breakfast.

2 tablespoons olive oil
8 ounces lean ground beef
1 small onion, finely chopped (⅓ cup)
1 clove garlic, minced
1 teaspoon dried oregano, crushed
1 large tomato, seeded
   and chopped (¾ cup)
   Kosher salt or table salt and freshly
   ground black pepper, to taste
6 eggs
¼ cup whipping cream
1 cup shredded cheddar
   cheese (4 ounces)
   Shredded cheddar cheese
   Shredded lettuce (optional)
   Chopped, seeded tomato (optional)

1 * Preheat the broiler. In an 8-inch nonstick broiler-safe skillet heat 1 tablespoon of the oil over high heat. Add the ground beef; cook for 4 to 5 minutes or until browned, breaking the meat up with a wooden spoon. Add the onion, garlic, and oregano; cook for 1 minute. Add the tomato and season with salt and pepper; cook for 1 minute more. Spoon the mixture onto a plate and let cool slightly. Wipe out the skillet with a paper towel.

2 * In a large bowl beat the eggs and cream; season with a little salt and pepper. Stir in the 1 cup shredded cheese and the beef mixture; mix well. Heat the remaining 1 tablespoon oil in the same skillet over medium-low heat. Add the egg mixture; cook for 5 to 6 minutes or until the edges are cooked and pull away from the sides of the pan.

3 * Transfer the pan to the broiler; broil for 3 to 4 minutes or until the eggs are set and lightly browned. Remove from the oven. Run a heatproof plastic spatula around the edges to loosen the frittata. Let it stand for a few minutes before inverting it onto a plate. Top with additional shredded cheese and, if desired, lettuce and tomato.

GEORGE'S SECRET ⌄

Instead of ground beef, try using hot sausage for a more fiery frittata.

POTATO CHIP SPANISH TORTILLA

PREP: 10 minutes / COOK: 5 minutes / BROIL: 3 minutes / YIELD: 4 servings

Here I share with you the famous potato chip recipe I told you about earlier in this chapter. Make this recipe more memorable by using thick-cut, gourmet chips and only the freshest eggs.

6   eggs
1   (5-ounce) bag high-end potato
        chips (such as Terra Chips),
        slightly crushed
1   large tomato, seeded and
        finely chopped (¾ cup)
½   of a yellow sweet pepper,
        finely chopped (⅓ cup)
3   tablespoons chopped green onion
1   tablespoon vegetable oil

1* Preheat the broiler. In a large bowl beat the eggs. Add the chips, tomato, sweet pepper, and green onion. Let stand for 5 to 10 minutes or until the chips have softened.

2* In a broiler-safe nonstick skillet heat the oil over medium-low heat. Add the egg mixture; cook slowly for 5 to 6 minutes or until the edges are cooked and pull away from the sides of the pan.

3* Transfer the pan to the broiler; broil for 3 to 4 minutes or until the eggs are set and lightly browned. Remove from the oven. Run a heatproof plastic spatula around the edges to loosen the tortilla. Let stand for a few minutes before serving.

If the handle of your skillet is made of plastic, simply wrap it with foil before placing it in the oven. Be sure your skillet is oven-safe (it should say so on the bottom of the pan or in the manufacturer's directions).

SUN-DRIED TOMATO CHEDDAR GRITS

PREP: 10 minutes / CHILL: 2 hours / COOK: 24 minutes / YIELD: 6 to 8 servings

Dried tomatoes give this Southern classic a savory twist. To save time,
I make the grits the night before. The next morning all I have to do
is slice, fry, and serve with some eggs. Then take a nap.

5   cups water
1   cup quick-cooking grits (not instant)
1   cup shredded sharp cheddar cheese
        (4 ounces)
¼   cup sun-dried tomato paste
1   teaspoon kosher salt or
        ¾ teaspoon table salt
     Nonstick cooking spray
1   tablespoon vegetable oil

1* In a saucepan bring the water to a boil over high heat; add the grits. Lower the heat to medium; simmer about 5 minutes, stirring frequently. Stir in the cheese, tomato paste, and salt. Turn off the heat and let stand for 2 minutes.

2* Coat a small loaf pan (9×5×2-inch) or mold (see below) with nonstick cooking spray. Pour in the grits mixture. Wrap with plastic wrap; chill in refrigerator at least 2 hours or overnight. Run a butter knife around the side of the pan; invert to remove the loaf from the pan. Use a wet knife to cut the loaf into ½-inch slices.

3* In a nonstick skillet heat the oil over medium-high heat. Fry each slice for 3 to 4 minutes on each side or until crispy and browned. Keep fried slices warm while you fry the rest.

HOLY GRAIL OF OPTIONS ⌄

SHAPES

STORAGE   SQUARES

PANS

You can use almost anything to mold the grits. Try flexible silicon molds, baking pans, plastic storage containers, old paint cans, etc. (Just kidding about the paint cans! Please don't sue me!)

BANANA SPLIT PANCAKES

PREP: 10 minutes / COOK: 20 minutes / YIELD: about 8 pancakes

Who said you can't have a banana split for breakfast? Okay, your mom did.
Consider this recipe a clever compromise that will remind your mother
how creative you are.

1   cup pancake mix
¾   cup milk
1   egg
1   tablespoon vegetable oil
4   ripe bananas
     Nonstick cooking spray
½   cup semisweet chocolate chips
     Chocolate sauce or maple syrup
     Whipped cream
     Maraschino cherries (optional)

1* In a bowl combine the pancake mix, milk, egg, and oil; mix well.
The batter should be the consistency of thick cream. Add more milk,
1 tablespoon at a time, if necessary, to reach the desired consistency.

2* Trim the ends of the bananas to make pieces about 4 inches
long. Slice the pieces in half lengthwise and crosswise. Mash the
banana ends and mix them into the batter.

3* Coat a nonstick skillet with nonstick cooking spray and heat
over medium-low heat for 2 to 3 minutes. Pour ⅓ cup batter into
the skillet. Gently press two pieces of banana into the batter. Scatter
some of the chocolate chips over the pancake. Cook until bubbles
form on the edges of the pancake and the bottom is golden brown.
Flip and cook the other side until it is golden brown. Remove from
pan and keep warm while you cook the rest of the pancakes.

4* Serve with chocolate sauce, whipped cream, and, if desired,
a cherry.

NOTE: For a giant stack of pancakes, just double, triple,
or quadruple the recipe!

This is what
the pancake
should look like.

RASPBERRY AND WHITE CHOCOLATE SOY PANCAKES

PREP: 10 minutes / COOK: 20 minutes / YIELD: 8 pancakes

These pancakes are delicious, but they do require some dexterity. The secret is to place individual white chocolate chips and raspberries on each pancake while the bottom is cooking.

1 cup pancake mix
¾ cup soymilk
1 egg
1 tablespoon vegetable oil
   Nonstick cooking spray
½ pint fresh raspberries
   (cut large berries in half)
½ cup white chocolate chips
   Maple syrup (optional)

1* In a medium bowl stir together the pancake mix, soymilk, egg, and oil. The batter should be the consistency of thick cream. Add more soymilk, 1 tablespoon at a time, if necessary, to reach the desired consistency.

2* Coat a nonstick skillet with nonstick cooking spray and heat over medium-low heat for 2 to 3 minutes. Pour ¼ cup batter into the skillet. Gently press some raspberries and white chocolate chips into the batter. Cook until bubbles form on the edge of the pancake and the bottom is golden brown. Flip and cook the other side until golden brown. Remove from the pan and keep warm while you cook the rest of the pancakes. If desired, serve with maple syrup.

MYSTERY THINGAMAJIGS ∨

What, you're too lazy even for pancake MIX? No problem, because with the aerosol power of a can of Batter Blaster, you can just *spray* your cakes right onto the griddle!

CORNMEAL CRUSTED FRENCH TOAST

PREP: 10 minutes / STAND: 15 minutes / COOK: 15 minutes / YIELD: 2 to 3 servings

Is there any food that wouldn't love a nice cornmeal crust? Okay, probably lettuce. But as for French toast, I think we may have found its soul mate!

3   eggs
½   cup milk
1   teaspoon vanilla
½   teaspoon kosher salt
        or ¼ teaspoon table salt
¼   teaspoon ground cinnamon
        Pinch ground nutmeg
6   (¾-inch) slices challah
        or other egg bread
½   cup cornmeal
2   to 3 tablespoons butter
        Maple syrup or honey
        Strawberries

1* In a large bowl beat the eggs with the milk, vanilla, salt, cinnamon, and nutmeg. Add the bread slices; let stand for 15 to 20 minutes or until the bread has absorbed the liquid.

2* Put the cornmeal in a shallow dish. Lightly coat the soaked bread slices with the cornmeal. In a nonstick skillet heat 1 tablespoon butter over medium heat. Working in batches and adding more butter as necessary, cook the bread for 2 to 3 minutes on each side or until golden brown. Serve with maple syrup or honey and garnish with strawberries.

SO THAT'S HOW YOU DO IT ⌄

To make an eye-catching strawberry garnish, simply place a large strawberry stem side down next to the handle of a wooden spoon. Then cut down vertically until you reach the spoon. Repeat in ⅛-inch-wide slices across the strawberry, then gently fan out and let the compliments roll in.

ORANGE CROISSANT FRENCH TOAST

PREP: 10 minutes / COOK: 10 minutes / YIELD: 4 servings

I don't know why, but smaller croissants just look classier than the large ones. If you can't find small ones, cut some large croissants in half and then stand across the room! They'll look smaller from a distance.

3   eggs
¼   cup milk
2   tablespoons sugar
1   teaspoon orange zest
2   tablespoons fresh orange juice
1   tablespoon orange liqueur (such
        as Cointreau) (optional)
2   to 3 tablespoons butter
12   small croissants or 6 large
        croissants, cut in half lengthwise
     Powdered sugar
     Orange zest (optional)
     Honey (optional)

1* In a shallow dish beat the eggs with the milk, sugar, 1 teaspoon zest, orange juice, and liqueur, if using. In a nonstick skillet melt 1 tablespoon of the butter over medium-low heat. Dip the croissant slices into the egg mixture until well coated. Cook in hot butter about 3 minutes per side or until golden brown. Work in batches, adding more butter as necessary. Sprinkle with powdered sugar. If desired, garnish with additional orange zest and serve with honey.

The key to perfect French toast is to use low heat and be very patient.

CHOCOLATE BREAKFAST

PREP: 15 minutes / COOK: 15 minutes / YIELD: 10 to 12 servings **SANDWICHES**

Feel free to experiment with other types of bread, fruits, nuts, and, of course, various chocolates. The slower these sandwiches cook, the meltier the chocolate will be!

1   Italian baguette or other dense bread
     Butter, softened
     Thin milk chocolate squares
       (recommended: Ghirardelli
       Chocolate Squares)
     Fresh fruit slices (such
       as strawberries, bananas,
       and raspberries)

1* Heat a griddle or a small skillet over medium heat. Slice the bread into ¼-inch slices. Butter one side of 2 slices of bread. Put the bread, buttered side down, on the griddle. Place a square of chocolate on top of one slice and top with some sliced fruit. Cover with the other slice of bread, buttered side up; cook on both sides until the chocolate is melted. Repeat with the remaining ingredients. Serve immediately.

HOLY GRAIL OF OPTIONS ⌄

JAM   FRUIT   CHOCOLATE

Put your own spin on this sandwich by varying the ingredients. Here are just a few of the many possible options.

frozen banana pops

PREP: 15 minutes
FREEZE: 4 hours
YIELD: 8 pops

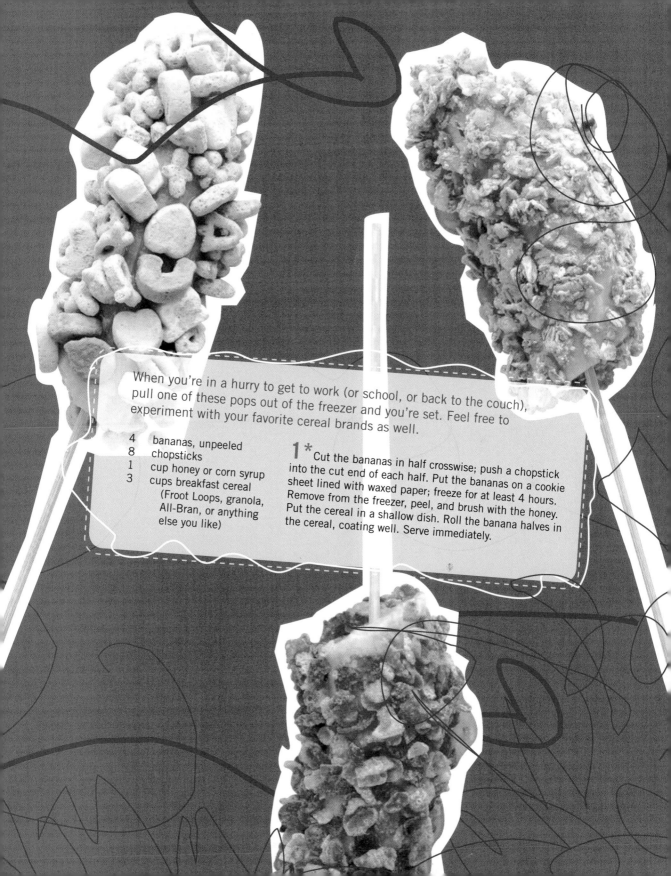

When you're in a hurry to get to work (or school, or back to the couch), pull one of these pops out of the freezer and you're set. Feel free to experiment with your favorite cereal brands as well.

4   bananas, unpeeled
8   chopsticks
1   cup honey or corn syrup
3   cups breakfast cereal
      (Froot Loops, granola,
      All-Bran, or anything
      else you like)

1* Cut the bananas in half crosswise; push a chopstick into the cut end of each half. Put the bananas on a cookie sheet lined with waxed paper; freeze for at least 4 hours. Remove from the freezer, peel, and brush with the honey. Put the cereal in a shallow dish. Roll the banana halves in the cereal, coating well. Serve immediately.

COFFEE MARSHMALLOW

CRISPY TREATS

PREP: 5 minutes / COOK: 8 minutes / YIELD: about 24 bars

If you live for your latte or cappuccino, this treat is right up your caffeinated alley. I like to take it from the slow-paced alley to the fast-paced freeway by tossing a few chopped chocolate-covered espresso beans into the mix.

3 tablespoons butter
1 (10-ounce) package
    miniature marshmallows
2 to 3 tablespoons instant
    coffee or espresso powder
6 cups rice cereal (recommended:
    Rice Krispies)

1 *Lightly butter an 8×8×2-inch baking pan. In a large pan melt the butter over very low heat. Stir in the marshmallows. Cook, stirring frequently, until the marshmallows are melted and smooth. Remove the pan from the heat. Stir in the instant coffee (2 tablespoons for a rich coffee flavor, 3 tablespoons for a real kick) and mix well. Gently stir in the rice cereal. When it is completely coated, use buttered hands to lightly press the mixture into the prepared pan. Cool and cut into bars.

NOTE: To make these treats into tall, fat cubes like the photo, place the rice cereal mixture into a terrine mold or other long, thin pan.

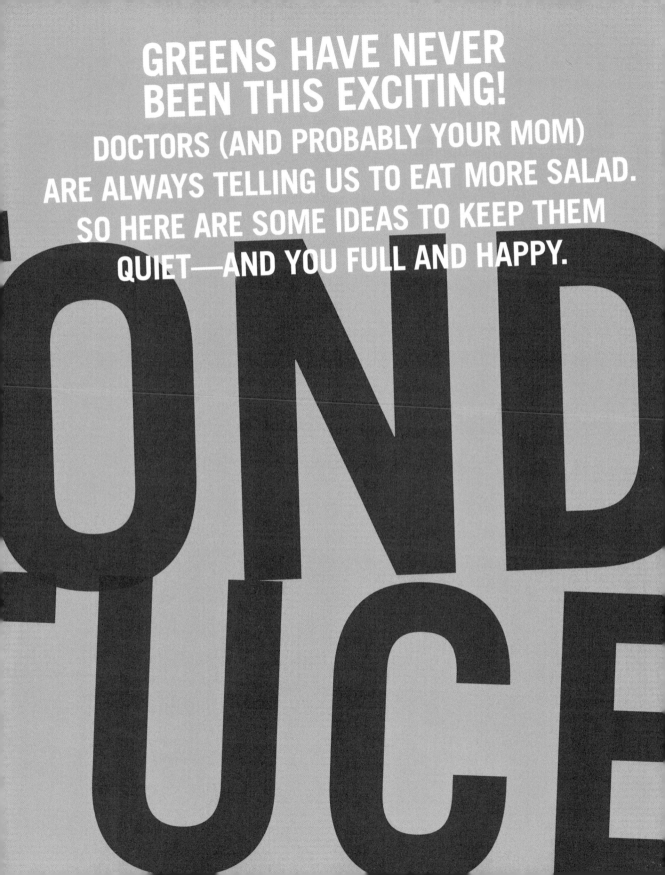

GREENS HAVE NEVER
BEEN THIS EXCITING!
DOCTORS (AND PROBABLY YOUR MOM)
ARE ALWAYS TELLING US TO EAT MORE SALAD.
SO HERE ARE SOME IDEAS TO KEEP THEM
QUIET—AND YOU FULL AND HAPPY.

BEWARE OF THE SNEEZE GUARD

One thing you should know about me: I love salad. And I hate it. Okay, technically that's a total contradiction! But I don't need to tell you that life, like salad, can sometimes be a contradiction.

The salad I *love* is the one that recalls my early childhood: salads made from fresh produce I'd procure on trips to the farmer's market in Caracas with my dad. Salads like my mom's Armenian tabouli salad.

The salad I *hate* is one that recalls the summer of 1990. I was en route to Asbury Park, New Jersey, with my friend Armand to see our preferred purveyors of thrash: Overkill. On the way, we stopped for some mosh-pit fuel. To our delight, every meal came with unlimited access to . . . the salad bar.

Yes, the salad bar. Those infamous pathogen incubators, where, instead of a bowl, they should supply diners with a petri dish. But these were rebellious times for yours truly. So I didn't mind that the iceberg lettuce sported a golden sheen or that the green olives looked brown while the blue cheese dressing was green. It was free! It was unlimited! And though the fresh, flavorful salads I'd grown up on were a symphony for the palate, all this hungry, head-banging teen wanted was some all-you-can-eat overkill.

It would, alas, be the only overkill I would experience that night. Once we got to the show, I endured three minutes of half-hearted moshing before that suspect salad sent me directly to the land of the "gastric disturbance." And while my metal phase endured for a couple more years, that night marked the end of my "salad bar phase." **It also provided me with entry #3 in Duran's Rules for Gastronomic Glee: "Man shall eat no salad where a sneeze guard is involved." Amen.**

GEORGE'S ARTICHOKE TUNA SALAD

PREP: 10 minutes / YIELD: 2 cups

With the flavorful zing of artichoke hearts and cilantro, this will be your
go-to tuna salad to serve on bread, lettuce, or just to eat on its own.

2   (6-ounce) cans solid white tuna
      (water pack), drained
1   cup mayonnaise
4   canned artichoke hearts, drained,
      squeezed, and chopped
2   green onions (white and
      green parts), chopped
2   tablespoons snipped fresh cilantro
1   tablespoon fresh lemon juice (plus
      more to taste, if desired)
6   dashes bottled hot pepper sauce
      Kosher salt or table salt and freshly
      ground black pepper, to taste

1 * In a medium bowl combine all the ingredients and mix well.
Taste and adjust the seasonings.

2 * Serving suggestions: Use as a sandwich filling for your favorite
bread. Make an open-face tuna melt by spreading the tuna mixture on
bread, topping with cheese, and broiling for a few minutes. Or mound
the tuna salad on cooked slices of eggplant or portobello mushrooms
for a breadless sandwich.

HOLY GRAIL OF OPTIONS ⌄

CANNED   FROZEN   JARRED   FRESH!

Small Artichoke Hearts

BIRDS EYE
ARTICHOKE HEARTS

Use any type
of artichoke
hearts for the
recipe, such as
canned, frozen,
jarred, or even
fresh (if you're
up for a little
extra work).

Crackin' Up: To serve, use salad tongs to break the tortillas into pieces and mix the salad.

HAPPY TACO SALAD

PREP: 20 minutes / BAKE: 3 minutes / YIELD: 4 to 6 servings

The best part of this salad? Serving it. When your guests see you breaking the tortillas into pieces, they might wonder exactly where this salad meal is headed. But once they taste it, they'll be happy to stay and eat!

5   (7-inch) flour tortillas
1   tablespoon olive oil
3   cups finely chopped iceberg lettuce
2   avocados, finely chopped
1   cup snipped fresh cilantro
2   ripe tomatoes, seeded and
     finely chopped
2   tablespoons extra virgin olive oil
1   tablespoon lime juice
1   teaspoon bottled hot pepper sauce
1   teaspoon Dijon-style mustard
     Kosher salt or table salt and freshly
     ground black pepper, to taste
2   cups shredded cooked chicken
1   cup shredded Tex-Mex cheese
     blend (4 ounces)
     Salsa (optional)

1 * Preheat the oven (or a toaster oven) to 350°F. Brush both sides of the tortillas with the olive oil. Place the tortillas on the oven rack and bake about 3 minutes or until they are puffed and golden brown. Set aside to cool.

2 * In a large bowl toss together the lettuce, avocado, cilantro, and tomato. In a small bowl whisk together the extra virgin olive oil, lime juice, hot pepper sauce, and mustard; season with salt and pepper. Pour over the salad and toss to mix.

3 * Place a crisp tortilla in the bottom of a large salad bowl. Cover with one-fourth of the lettuce mixture, one-fourth of the chicken, and one-fourth of the cheese. Layer the tortilla, salad, chicken, and cheese three more times. If desired, top with salsa and additional shredded cheese.

4 * To serve, use salad tongs to crack the tortillas into pieces and mix the salad.

HOLY GRAIL OF OPTIONS ⌄

OLIVES   JALAPEÑOS   BEANS   PORK

To put your signature on this salad, add some variety. Need some suggestions? Try chopped olives, pickled jalapeños, rinsed black beans, or even pulled pork!

spoon-friendly cobb salad

PREP: 15 minutes
YIELD: 4 to 6 servings

Hey, you—put that fork down! For me, a true Cobb salad should be eaten with a spoon. And with a light vinaigrette, you'll be able to taste all the components without overwhelming your palate.

2	tablespoons red wine vinegar	1	cup finely chopped cooked chicken or turkey
2	tablespoons extra virgin olive oil	2	ripe avocados, finely chopped
1	tablespoon Dijon-style mustard Kosher salt or table salt and freshly ground black pepper, to taste	2	large tomatoes, seeded and finely chopped (1½ cups)
		4	ounces blue cheese, crumbled (1 cup)
1	head iceberg lettuce, finely shredded	8	slices cooked bacon, crumbled
		2	hard-cooked eggs, finely chopped

1* For the vinaigrette, in a small bowl whisk together the vinegar, oil, and mustard; season with salt and pepper. Arrange lettuce in the center of a large platter. Arrange the remaining ingredients in piles around the lettuce.

Spinach is a rich source of iron! Or is it? Many believe this misconception was born in 1870, when Dr. E. von Wolf misplaced a decimal point in a scientific publication. The result was a figure for iron that was ten times too high!

CAESAR SPINACH SALAD

PREP: 10 minutes / COOK: 5 minutes / YIELD: 2 to 4 servings

I know what you're thinking: Anchovies? Believe me, you have nothing to fear.
Once the anchovies are mixed into the dressing, you'll forget all about them.
All you'll remember is genuine Caesar salad flavor and delight.

4	slices sandwich bread
1	tablespoon vegetable oil
2	cloves garlic, crushed
3	anchovies
	Juice of 1 lemon
1	teaspoon Dijon-style mustard
2	cloves garlic, forced through a garlic press or finely chopped
	Kosher salt or table salt and freshly ground black pepper, to taste
2	tablespoons extra virgin olive oil
1	(6-ounce) bag baby spinach
2	tablespoons freshly grated Parmesan cheese
	Crispy Parmesan Bowls

1 * For the croutons, trim the crusts off the bread slices and discard. Cut the remaining bread into cubes. In a skillet heat the vegetable oil over medium-high heat. Add the crushed garlic and cook until lightly browned. Remove and discard the garlic. Add the bread cubes and increase the heat to high. Cook the cubes until they are well browned. Drain on paper towels.

2 * For the dressing, in a large salad bowl crush the anchovies with a fork until they form a paste. Add the lemon juice, mustard, and garlic; season with salt and pepper. Whisk together well, then whisk in the olive oil.

3 * Add the spinach, Parmesan, and croutons to the dressing. Toss well and serve immediately in Crispy Parmesan Bowls.

CRISPY PARMESAN BOWLS: In a large nonstick skillet spread ¼ cup freshly grated Parmesan cheese evenly over the bottom to form a 7-inch circle. Cook over medium heat until the cheese is bubbly and lightly browned, about 3 minutes. Remove the pan from the heat. Put a small bowl upside down on a cutting board. When the bubbling stops (about 1 minute), carefully remove the cheese disk with a thin metal spatula and drape it over the bowl. Press gently with the spatula so it forms a bowl. (Be careful—it is fragile.) Repeat process three more times to form 4 bowls. Let the Parmesan bowls cool completely. Put the Parmesan bowls on plates; fill each with 2 cups of the Caesar Spinach Salad.

SO THAT'S HOW YOU DO IT ⌄

Want to really impress your guests? When you are making the Parmesan bowls, use a rolling pin to make a thin strip of melted Parmesan. Press the strip on a rolling pin so that it curls into a C shape. Let cool and serve on the salad.

LAYERED CAPRESE SALAD

PREP: 10 minutes / YIELD: 2 servings

This classic salad has a new look—layers! It's easy to assemble and brings
a fresh splash of quintessentially Italian colors and flavors to any meal.
Having extra guests over? This recipe easily doubles and triples.

2   large red or yellow tomatoes
1   (8-ounce) ball fresh mozzarella,
     sliced into 4 pieces
4   tablespoons basil pesto
1   cup fresh basil leaves,
     cut into thin strips
   Extra virgin olive oil
   Fleur de sel or sea salt

1 *Bring a small pan of water to a boil. Fill a large bowl with cold water and ice. Remove the tomato stems and cut a small X in the bottom of each tomato. Gently lower the tomatoes into the boiling water for 5 to 10 seconds or until the skins start to peel. Immediately remove the tomatoes and submerge them in the ice water. Slip the skins off the tomatoes. Cut each tomato crosswise into three slices.

2 *Put the bottom slice of a tomato on a plate. Top with a slice of mozzarella, 1 tablespoon pesto, and 1 tablespoon basil. Continue layering, ending with the top of the tomato. Do the same with the second tomato. Drizzle with olive oil and sprinkle with fleur de sel.

HOLY GRAIL OF OPTIONS ⌄

WHITE

CURRY

OLIVE

MEDITERRANEAN

Fleur de sel is the caviar of salts. This gray sea salt is harvested by hand by workers who scrape the top layer of salt before it sinks to the bottom of large pans. Sprinkle it on food— never cook with it!

CREAMY TOMATO AND GOAT CHEESE

SALAD

PREP: 15 minutes / STAND: 30 minutes / YIELD: 4 to 6 servings

Sometimes you just get lucky. One day I accidentally let some diced tomatoes and goat cheese rest for a bit and discovered that I'd "invented" a tomato salad with a creamy, succulent dressing. The colors will hook you even before the first bite.

3   large tomatoes (about 2 pounds)
8   ounces fresh goat cheese, crumbled
1   cup fresh basil, chopped
1   large shallot, finely chopped
      (about 3 tablespoons)
2   tablespoons extra virgin olive oil
2   tablespoons lemon juice
      Kosher salt or table salt and freshly
         ground black pepper, to taste

1 * Bring a small pan of water to a boil. Fill a large bowl with cold water and ice. Remove the tomato stems and cut a small X in the bottom of each tomato. Gently lower the tomatoes into the boiling water for 5 to 10 seconds or until the skins start to peel. Immediately remove the tomatoes and submerge them in the ice water. Slip the skins off the tomatoes.

2 * Cut the tomatoes into large chunks and put them in a large salad bowl. Add the goat cheese, basil, shallot, oil, and lemon juice; season with salt and pepper. Toss gently and let stand, covered, at room temperature for 30 minutes. Toss again. The goat cheese and tomato juice will have made a creamy dressing. Serve at room temperature.

feta

goat

Can't find goat cheese? Simply replace it with the same amount of fabulous feta cheese!

WALDORF SALAD-STUFFED ENDIVES

PREP: 10 minutes / COOK: 10 minutes / COOL: 1 hour / YIELD: 4 to 5 appetizer servings

This one goes out to all you Waldorf lovers. I know you're out there! Now, thanks to the miracle of Belgian endive, you can share your love of Waldorf at your next party by turning this timeless classic into finger food.

½ cup sugar
1 tablespoon water
½ cup chopped walnuts
2 endives
1 Anjou pear, cut into
  matchstick-size strips
4 ounces Gorgonzola cheese,
  crumbled (1 cup)
1 to 2 tablespoons balsamic glaze

1* In a nonstick skillet cook the sugar and water over high heat, stirring constantly. When the sugar syrup begins to brown, add the nuts; mix until evenly coated. Remove from the heat. Spread the nuts on a cookie sheet lined with waxed paper. Cool completely. Coarsely chop the nuts.

2* Separate the endive leaves; use the best and largest ones. Put some pear, gorgonzola, and caramelized walnuts on each leaf. Drizzle a serving plate with the balsamic glaze. Arrange stuffed leaves over the drizzle on the serving plate. Serve immediately.

NOTE: Balsamic glaze is available in many supermarkets, but if you can't find it, make your own by slowly simmering 1 cup of balsamic vinegar for about an hour until it has a thick, syrupy consistency.

HOLY GRAIL OF OPTIONS ⌄

ORANGES

APPLES

GRAPES

POMEGRANATE SEEDS

In my Waldorf salad I use Anjou pears as the fruit component. But it's easy to replace them with a fruit of your choice. Try apples, oranges, grapes, even pomegranate seeds!

STRAWBERRY ARUGULA SALAD

PREP: 15 minutes / COOK: 5 minutes / YIELD: 4 servings

Fruit in salads is one of my favorites. Here the sweetness of the strawberries contrasts perfectly with the peppery arugula, and the balsamic vinegar's complex flavor brings the two tastily together.

½ cup pine nuts
1 (6-ounce) bag arugula
1 cup fresh mint leaves
½ cup strawberries, hulled and sliced
4 ounces mild fresh goat cheese, crumbled (1 cup)
1 tablespoon honey
2 teaspoons lemon juice
2 teaspoons balsamic vinegar
2 tablespoons extra virgin olive oil
  Kosher salt or table salt and freshly ground black pepper, to taste

1* In a small skillet toast the pine nuts over medium heat for 5 to 6 minutes or until they are golden brown, stirring often.

2* Put the arugula and mint leaves in a large salad bowl. Add the strawberries and goat cheese. In a small bowl whisk together the honey, lemon juice, and vinegar; whisk in the olive oil and season with salt and pepper. Pour the dressing over the salad and toss well. Top with toasted pine nuts; serve immediately.

SO THAT'S HOW YOU DO IT ⌄

Want to look like a real chef? Then you need to learn the art of the pan toss. You can practice with the pine nuts in this recipe. Hold the pan at a 30-degree angle and let nuts come down to the edge without falling. In one clean motion, jerk the pan toward you, allowing the nuts to spring back to the center of the pan.

MESCLUN, PROSCIUTTO, AND MELON SALAD

PREP: 10 minutes / COOK: 5 minutes / YIELD: 4 servings

Attention, all chefs: Start your ballers! This sweet, earthy, and tastily tangy fruit salad is all about getting your mel-on!

1 tablespoon olive oil
1 cup chopped prosciutto
    (about 6 slices)
2 teaspoons orange juice
1 tablespoon red wine vinegar
2 tablespoons extra virgin olive oil
1 tablespoon finely chopped
    shallot or chives
  Kosher salt or table salt and freshly
    ground black pepper, to taste
4 cups mesclun salad mix
1 cup cantaloupe balls or cubes
4 wooden skewers (optional)

1* In a nonstick skillet heat the 1 tablespoon olive oil over medium-high heat. Add chopped prosciutto; cook for 5 to 7 minutes or until crispy. Drain on paper towels.

2* For dressing, whisk together the orange juice, vinegar, extra virgin olive oil, and shallot. Taste and adjust the seasoning with salt and pepper.

3* Set some of the dressing aside. Toss the remaining dressing with the salad greens and divide among 4 bowls. If desired, thread some cantaloupe balls on each of the skewers (or just add them to the salad without the skewers). Top each bowl with prosciutto and drizzle with the reserved dressing.

HOLY GRAIL OF OPTIONS ⌄

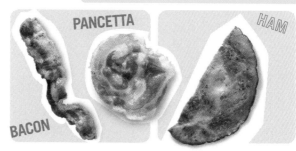

PANCETTA

HAM

BACON

You can replace the prosciutto with bacon, pancetta, or any thickly sliced dry-cured ham.

FROM
TO
MINUS T

SOUP ISN'T JUST FOR WINTER! FROM COLD SOUPS TO DESSERT SOUPS, I HAVE FLAVORFUL RECIPES FOR EVERY SEASON AND EVERY MOOD. AND WITH PREMADE STOCK AVAILABLE IN ALL SUPERMARKETS, PREP TIME IS CUT IN HALF.

THE CHICKEN NOODLE SOUP-OFF

My mom makes the best chicken noodle soup in the world. END OF STORY. Well, actually, it's the beginning of the story.

To be honest, pretty much every Armenian kid claims their mom or grandmother makes "the BEST [fill in the blank] in the world." But my mom's chicken noodle soup *actually is the best in the world*! Combining only the freshest ingredients and cooked to perfection in a pressure cooker, it's the one recipe of hers I had never even dared to try to duplicate (possibly because pressure cookers kind of scare me!).

Don't believe me? Well, neither did my friends Armand and Vache, who once went a little too far with the trash talk, claiming that *their* grandmother's soup took top prize. It was a silly mistake, followed by a fatal error: accepting my challenge to settle it in a good old-fashioned chicken noodle soup-off!

In a gathering that would provide the initial spark for the creation of *Ham on the Street,* we drafted three friends to "sip in judgment" of the two soups, side by side, while blindfolded. The air was thick with tension. Fortunately it was also thick with the overwhelmingly soothing aroma of chicken noodle soup, which alleviated any chance of fisticuffs once the verdict was rendered.

And while I was supremely confident that my mom's soup knew no peer, I will admit to some small twinges of nervousness as the judges spent what seemed like an eternity in deliberation. Finally, in a room so quiet you could have heard the proverbial pin drop, they emerged to reveal the unanimous champion: MY MOM'S SOUP!

Even though I knew hers was the best all along, it felt good to have a little "official" confirmation. And while I won't be hearing any more trash talk from Armand and Vache, I can't help wondering if any of you might be thinking how your mom's soup might measure up. To you I offer a simple invitation: Meet me at the Soup-Off!

PEPPERONI PIZZA SOUP

PREP: 15 minutes / COOK: 6 minutes / BROIL: 3 minutes / YIELD: 4 servings

Finally, liquid food lovers everywhere can rejoice. America's favorite pizza is ready for sipping! Remember to try different "toppings" as well, such as mushrooms, onions, and sausage!

2 (10.75-ounce) cans condensed tomato soup
3 cups water
2 cloves garlic, minced
1½ cups dried elbow macaroni (or other short dried pasta such as ditalini or alphabets)
2 green onions, sliced
2 teaspoons dried oregano, crushed
⅓ cup diced pepperoni
1 cup shredded mozzarella cheese (4 ounces)
1 cup shredded cheddar cheese (4 ounces)
   Dried oregano

1 *Preheat the broiler. In a large pan put the tomato soup, water, and garlic; bring to a boil over high heat. Stir in the macaroni, green onion, oregano, and pepperoni; cook for 6 to 8 minutes or until the macaroni is almost done. Pour the soup into 4 oven-proof bowls. Top each with ¼ cup mozzarella cheese, ¼ cup cheddar cheese, and some oregano. Broil for 3 to 5 minutes or until the cheese is bubbly and lightly browned. (Or serve the soup in a small round, crusty loaf of bread. Cut the top off the bread and scoop out the insides. Fill with soup, top with the cheeses, and broil as directed above.)

Need a nice wine to complement your pizza? Look no further. An Ohio-based company has come out with numerous choices under the name Pizza Vino.

PESTO PASTA SOUP

PREP: 15 minutes / COOK: 14 minutes / YIELD: 6 servings

One of my many mottos is "If it's got pesto—I'm in." A delicious dollop of the stuff in the center of this vegetable and pasta soup is the ultimate jumpstart into the fantastic flavor combinations that await.

2   tablespoons olive oil
1   medium onion, finely
      chopped (½ cup)
2   cloves garlic, minced
2   cups chopped carrot
1   cup chopped celery (2 stalks)
6   cups chicken stock or broth
2   cups dried medium shell pasta
1   cup snipped fresh basil
6   tablespoons basil pesto
    Shredded Parmesan cheese (optional)

1 * In a large pan heat the oil over medium-high heat. Add the onion and garlic; cook for 5 to 6 minutes or until the onions are soft and translucent. Add the carrot and celery; cook for 1 minute. Add the chicken stock and bring to a boil. Add the pasta and return to a boil. Lower the heat and simmer for 8 to 10 minutes or until the pasta is done, stirring occasionally. Skim off any foamy starch that appears on the surface. Remove from the heat and stir in the basil. Ladle into bowls; garnish with a tablespoon of pesto. If desired, sprinkle with shredded Parmesan cheese.

Go gourmet by making your own pesto. Simply process 2 cups of basil leaves with ½ cup grated Parmesan cheese, 2 cloves garlic, 3 tablespoons pine nuts, salt, and pepper. Drizzle in about ½ cup of extra virgin olive oil.

CHUNKY CHEDDAR CHILI

PREP: 15 minutes / COOK: 15 minutes / YIELD: 6 to 8 servings

Get the full alliteration effect by making this with David Bowie's "Ch-ch-ch-ch-chaaaaannnnggges" as your soundtrack. Then eat it up! Wash it down with some of the beer that is my secret (well, until now) weapon for updating this American comfort classic.

2   tablespoons butter
1   large onion, chopped (1 cup)
1   green sweet pepper, chopped
       (¾ cup)
2   (15.5-ounce) cans red
       kidney beans, drained
2   (14.5-ounce) cans diced
       tomatoes, drained
1   cup stout (such as Guinness)
1   tablespoon ground cumin
1   tablespoon dried oregano, crushed
1   teaspoon cayenne pepper
1   (10-ounce) package frozen
       chopped broccoli, thawed
4   cups shredded extra sharp
       cheddar cheese (16 ounces)
    Kosher salt or table salt and freshly
       ground black pepper, to taste
    Sour cream (optional)
    Shredded extra sharp cheddar
       cheese (optional)

1 *** In a large pan heat the butter over medium-high heat. Add the onion and sweet pepper; cook for 5 to 6 minutes or until the onion is translucent. Add the beans, tomatoes, stout, cumin, oregano, and cayenne pepper; bring to a boil. Add the broccoli. Lower the heat and simmer for 5 minutes. Stir in the cheese. Season with salt and pepper. If desired, serve with sour cream and additional shredded cheese.

How spicy do you like your chili? Try some of these amusing bottles of hot sauce in your batch. But be warned: These suckers are HOT. No joke.

Coconut-phobics, fear not. You can replace coconut milk with half-and-half or evaporated milk.

COCONUT LENTIL SOUP

PREP: 10 minutes / COOK: 30 minutes / YIELD: 6 servings

The tropical taste of coconut makes a tasty teammate for the uberversatile, always appetizing lentil. Alternate your sips with bites of this unique take on garlic bread and you have yourself some one-of-a-kind, cold-weather comfort.

2	tablespoons olive oil
1	medium onion, chopped (½ cup)
3	cloves garlic, crushed
2	tablespoons peeled and finely chopped fresh ginger
1	tablespoon ground cumin
1	tablespoon curry powder
2	cups red lentils
6	cups chicken stock or broth
2	cups unsweetened coconut milk
	Kosher salt or table salt and freshly ground black pepper, to taste
¼	cup snipped fresh cilantro
	Swiss Cilantro Garlic Bread

1 * In a large saucepan heat the oil over medium-high heat. Add the onion, garlic, ginger, cumin, and curry powder; cook for 3 to 4 minutes or until the onion is softened. Add the lentils and chicken stock and bring to a boil. Lower the heat and simmer, partially covered, about 10 minutes or until the lentils are tender. Add the coconut milk and season with salt and pepper; simmer for 10 minutes more. Just before serving, add the cilantro. Serve with warm Swiss Cilantro Garlic Bread.

SWISS CILANTRO GARLIC BREAD: Toast 6 thick bread slices and set aside. In a small bowl mix 1 cup shredded Swiss cheese, 3 tablespoons mayonnaise, 2 teaspoons snipped fresh cilantro, and 2 cloves garlic, minced. Spread the cheese mixture on the toasted bread. Broil or bake in a toaster oven for 2 to 3 minutes or until the cheese is melted and bubbly. Serve with soup.

HOLY GRAIL OF OPTIONS ⌄

MOZZARELLA & BASIL

GRUYÈRE & THYME

JARLSBERG & SAGE

For the garlic bread, try mozzarella, Gruyère, or Jarlsberg cheese with basil, thyme, or sage!

COMFY BUTTERNUT SQUASH SOUP

PREP: 15 minutes / COOK: 30 minutes / YIELD: 8 servings

You don't need a moonlit snowy night to appreciate
a batch of this soup (but it does help).

2   tablespoons olive oil
2   large onions, chopped (2 cups)
1   tablespoon curry powder
1   teaspoon ground cumin
1   teaspoon ground cinnamon
      Kosher salt or table salt and freshly
         ground black pepper, to taste
2   pounds butternut squash, peeled
         and cut into cubes
1   pound acorn squash, peeled
         and cut into cubes
8   sprigs fresh thyme
6   cups chicken stock or broth
2   cups water
1   (14-ounce) can unsweetened
         coconut milk
      Croutons
      Ground cinnamon (optional)
      Fresh thyme sprigs (optional)

1 * In a large saucepan heat the oil over medium-high heat. Add
the onions; cook for 5 to 6 minutes or until soft and translucent. Stir
in the curry, cumin, cinnamon, salt, and pepper; cook for 1 minute.
Add the squash, thyme, stock, and water. Bring to a boil; lower the
heat. Simmer about 20 minutes or until the squash is soft. Remove
the thyme sprigs. Using an immersion blender, or working in batches
with a regular blender, puree the soup until smooth and creamy. Add
the coconut milk. Season with additional salt and pepper to taste.
Ladle into soup bowls and top with croutons. If desired, garnish with
cinnamon and thyme sprigs.

SO THAT'S HOW YOU DO IT ⌄

Butternut squash
can be tough to cut.
Here's a tip to make it
easier: Place squash
in the microwave and
cook on high for 2 to
3 minutes to soften the
skin. Cut off the ends
of the squash. Use a
vegetable peeler to
remove the peel.

SOUPED-UP CARROT SOUP

PREP: 15 minutes / COOK: 25 minutes / YIELD: 4 servings

Ginger and honey are the secrets that make this
the number one requested soup among my friends.

2   tablespoons butter
2   cups chopped leeks (2 to 3 large)
3   tablespoons finely chopped
        fresh ginger
3   cloves garlic
3   cups chopped carrots (about 1 pound)
½   teaspoon ground allspice
½   teaspoon ground cinnamon
3   cups chicken stock or broth
2   cups water
2   tablespoons honey
     Kosher salt or table salt and freshly
        ground black pepper, to taste
     Carrot curls (optional)

1 * In a large pan heat the butter over medium-high heat. Add the
leeks, ginger, and garlic; cook for 5 to 6 minutes or until the leeks
are soft. Add the carrots, allspice, and cinnamon; stir well to combine.
Add the stock and water. Bring to a boil; lower the heat. Simmer for
10 to 12 minutes or until the carrots are soft. Skim off any foam that
may form. Using an immersion blender or working in batches with a
regular blender, puree the soup until smooth. Return the soup to the
heat and stir in the honey. Adjust the seasoning with salt and pepper.
If desired, serve garnished with carrot curls.

Useless Fact: Researchers are now breeding
carrots in different colors, each with
different nutritional benefits—all to get
you, the consumer, to eat more carrots!

ROASTED GARLIC SOUP

PREP: 15 minutes / ROAST: 30 minutes / COOK: 30 minutes / YIELD: 4 servings

There's nothing quite like the savory sweetness of roasted garlic. Although it's the ideal accent to many memorable dishes, this soup makes it the star attraction.

3   bulbs garlic
3   teaspoons olive oil
4   slices sandwich bread
1   tablespoon vegetable oil
2   cloves garlic, crushed
2   tablespoons butter
1   medium onion, finely
        chopped (½ cup)
2   teaspoons paprika
½   teaspoon ground cumin
4   cups vegetable or chicken
        stock or broth
     Snipped fresh parsley

1 * To roast the garlic, preheat the oven to 400°F. Cut the tops off the garlic bulbs. Wrap the bulbs with foil, leaving the cut edges exposed. Drizzle the olive oil over the garlic. Roast for 30 to 40 minutes or until the garlic is golden brown and soft. Remove from the oven. When cool enough to handle, squeeze the soft garlic into a small bowl; set aside.

2 * Meanwhile, for the croutons, trim the crusts off the bread slices and discard. Cut the remaining bread into small cubes. In a skillet heat the vegetable oil over medium-high heat. Add the crushed garlic; cook until lightly browned. Remove and discard the garlic. Add the bread cubes and increase the heat to high. Cook the cubes until they are well browned. Drain on paper towels.

3 * For the soup, melt the butter in a large pan over medium-high heat. Add the onion and cook for 5 to 6 minutes or until it is soft and translucent. Stir in the paprika, cumin, and roasted garlic. Add the stock and bring to a boil. Lower the heat and simmer for 15 minutes. Serve with croutons and snipped parsley.

SO THAT'S HOW YOU DO IT ⌄

Roasting garlic makes the bulb's strong taste more mild and sweet. Cut off the top of the bulb and place it in a nest of foil. Drizzle bulb with about one teaspoon olive oil. Bake in a 400°F oven for 30 to 40 minutes, until the garlic is soft and caramelized.

HERBED RED ONION SOUP

PREP: 15 minutes / COOK: 35 minutes / BROIL: 1 minute / YIELD: 4 servings

This tasty variation on the classically French onion soup gets its bold splash of color—and a deliciously sweet flavor—from red onions and red wine.

½ cup butter (1 stick)
4 large red onions, thinly sliced
2 teaspoons sugar
1 cup dry red wine
4 cups beef stock or broth
2 tablespoons fresh thyme
  Kosher salt or table salt and freshly
    ground black pepper, to taste
8 thick slices Italian bread
2 cups grated Gruyère and/or
    Swiss cheese (8 ounces)
  Snipped fresh thyme

1* In a large pan heat the butter over medium-low heat. Add the onions and sugar; cook for 20 to 25 minutes or until the onions are very brown and caramelized, stirring frequently. Add the wine and bring to a boil. Add the beef stock, thyme, salt, and pepper. Bring to a boil; lower the heat. Simmer for 10 minutes. Adjust the seasoning with salt and pepper.

2* While the soup is cooking, preheat the broiler. Toast the bread slices on both sides.

3* Pour the hot soup into 4 ovenproof bowls. Place 2 slices of toast on top of each and sprinkle ½ cup cheese evenly over the bread. Sprinkle with thyme. Broil for 1 to 2 minutes or until the cheese is bubbly and lightly browned. Serve immediately.

Do you get all choked up when you cut onions? Dry those tears and stop the sadness with these onion goggles!

berry good gazpacho

PREP: 10 minutes
YIELD: 4 servings

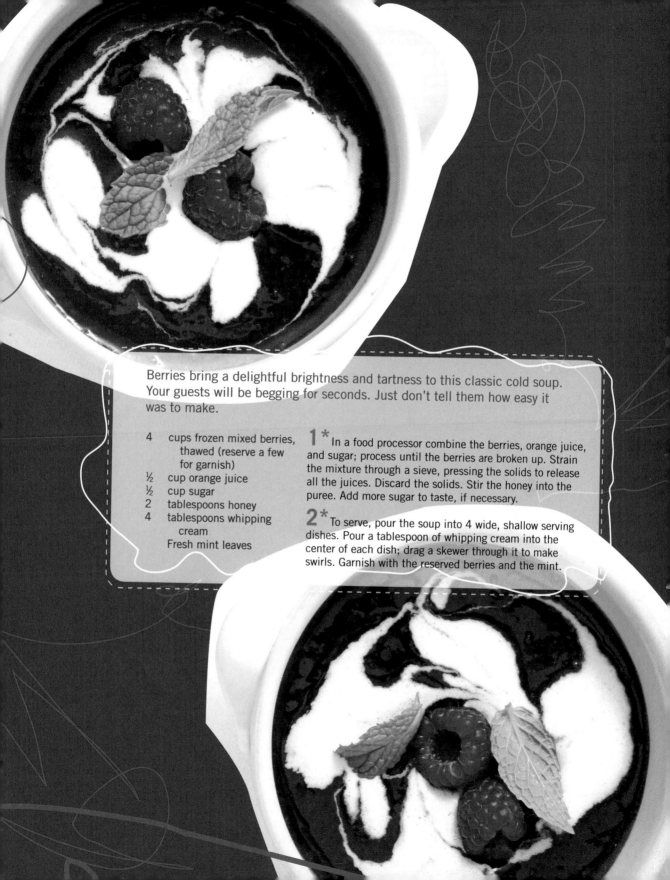

Berries bring a delightful brightness and tartness to this classic cold soup. Your guests will be begging for seconds. Just don't tell them how easy it was to make.

4 cups frozen mixed berries, thawed (reserve a few for garnish)
½ cup orange juice
½ cup sugar
2 tablespoons honey
4 tablespoons whipping cream
  Fresh mint leaves

1* In a food processor combine the berries, orange juice, and sugar; process until the berries are broken up. Strain the mixture through a sieve, pressing the solids to release all the juices. Discard the solids. Stir the honey into the puree. Add more sugar to taste, if necessary.

2* To serve, pour the soup into 4 wide, shallow serving dishes. Pour a tablespoon of whipping cream into the center of each dish; drag a skewer through it to make swirls. Garnish with the reserved berries and the mint.

CHOCOLATE SOUP

PREP: 10 minutes / STEEP: 20 minutes / COOK: 15 minutes / YIELD: 4 servings

I love soup. I love chocolate. Combining them into one scrumptiously self-indulgent dessert soup was what I was born to do. This soup is like hot chocolate that's so thick and rich you need a spoon to eat it. It may not cure your cold, but it certainly will warm your heart.

4½ cups milk
1 cup sweetened condensed milk
1 vanilla bean, split and scraped
10 ounces bittersweet chocolate, chopped
5 tablespoons cornstarch
5 tablespoons cold water
 Whipped cream (optional)
 Chocolate shavings (optional)
 Biscotti cookies (optional)
 Fresh raspberries (optional)

1 * In a medium saucepan over medium heat stir together the milk, sweetened condensed milk, and vanilla bean. Bring the mixture almost to a boil, stirring constantly. Remove from the heat and let steep for 20 minutes. Strain and return milk mixture to the pan. (Rinse and dry the vanilla bean and save it for another use.)

2 * Over low heat add the chocolate; whisk until the chocolate melts. Stir together the cornstarch and water; add to the chocolate mixture a little at a time, cooking and whisking constantly for 5 to 7 minutes or until the soup is thick and smooth. Pour the soup into bowls. If desired, pipe a swirl of whipped cream on the soup and garnish with chocolate shavings. If desired, serve with biscotti cookies and raspberries.

Are you the type that requires croutons with your soup? Then try serving this soup with chopped biscotti!

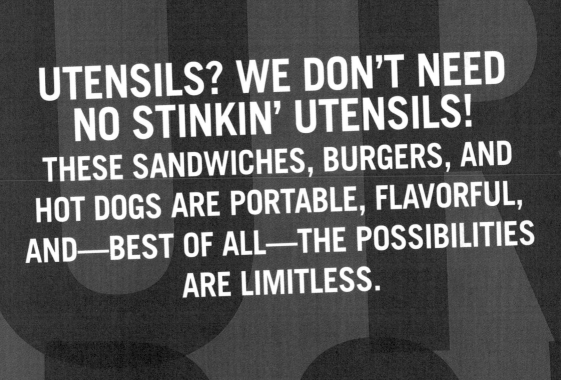

UTENSILS? WE DON'T NEED NO STINKIN' UTENSILS! THESE SANDWICHES, BURGERS, AND HOT DOGS ARE PORTABLE, FLAVORFUL, AND—BEST OF ALL—THE POSSIBILITIES ARE LIMITLESS.

ME AGAINST THE DOGS

I love any food you can eat with your hands. But for me, there's only one King, Kaiser, Khan of handheld cuisine. I speak, of course, of the humble hot dog.

Mine is a love affair born on the streets of Caracas, where I cut my culinary teeth on my country's mouthwatering contribution to tube steak history. A thin, salty, all-pork dog, swaddled in a melt-in-your-mouth steamed bun and finished with ketchup, mustard, mayo—plus the satisfying crunch of chopped cabbage and crushed potato chips. The Venezuelan hot dog is a one-of-a-kind delight that demands to be eaten by the truckload.

Years later all that experience had me feeling supremely confident when we shot the premiere episode of *Ham on the Street*. The bit was simple: I sat at a bus stop—cooking and offering up hot dogs to anyone who happened by. For the three-hour shoot, I figured I could eat 10 to 15 hot dogs—no problem. Or 20. Okay, 25!

But that giddiness quickly turned to gloom. After a mere half hour and four—four!—dogs, I was convinced I was going to die. Instead of the thin franks of my Venezuelan youth, these were bigger, beefy, American-style ones. In place of those melt-in-your mouth steamed buns, I was wrestling with the dry, bready, stomach-filling variety. So I closed my eyes and transported myself back to childhood. Back then, whenever any of my friends or I felt we had reached our limit, the rest would gather around him, quietly urging: "Otro . . . otro . . . otro . . . OTRO!" (meaning "one more").

Those words allowed me to somehow eat three more hot dogs and walk away unscathed. Yes, it's lame compared to the world record (66 dogs in 12 minutes!), but those guys? They're freaks! I'm just a guy who loves hot dogs—in moderation.

BLUE CHEESE BACON BURGERS

FREEZE: 1 hour / PREP: 15 minutes / GRILL: 8 minutes / YIELD: 4 burgers

Problem: Many blue cheese burgers I've had (and I've had a lot) lose the signature ingredient's one-of-a-kind sharpness when it melts into the burger. Solution? By freezing the blue cheese cubes and stuffing them in the burger, I'm guaranteed a solid chunk of that luscious cheese with each bite.

4   thick slices blue cheese
        (about 8 ounces)
1½   pounds ground beef chuck
½   pound ground pork
1   medium onion, finely
        chopped (½ cup)
1   cup chopped cooked
        bacon (about 6 slices)
3   tablespoons sun-dried tomato paste
¼   teaspoon liquid smoke
     Kosher salt or table salt and freshly
        ground black pepper, to taste
4   hamburger buns, toasted
     Lettuce
     Tomato slices
     Mayonnaise (optional)

1 * Freeze the cheese about 1 hour. Preheat a charcoal or gas grill to medium-high heat.

2 * In a large bowl combine the beef, pork, onion, bacon, tomato paste, and liquid smoke; season generously with salt and pepper. Mix together with your hands until well combined.

3 * Using your hands, form about one-fourth of the meat mixture into a ball. Make an indentation in the center. Put a slice of the frozen blue cheese into it; mold the burger around it to form a patty. Repeat with the rest of the meat mixture and cheese.

4 * Grill the patties directly over medium-high heat for 8 to 10 minutes or until done (160°F), turning once. (Or cook in a large nonstick skillet over medium-high heat for 8 to 10 minutes or until done [160°F].) Serve on hamburger buns with lettuce and tomato. If desired, add mayonnaise.

HOLY GRAIL OF OPTIONS ⌄

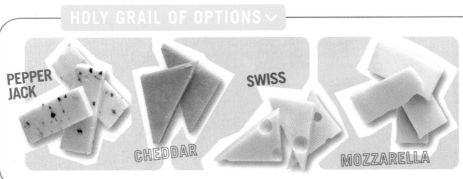

PEPPER JACK

CHEDDAR

SWISS

MOZZARELLA

Not a fan of blue cheese? No problem. Try freezing and stuffing cubes of pepper Jack, cheddar, Swiss, or mozzarella cheese into your next burger.

Added bonus of making this burger?
Sounding all gourmet at your next party
when you pronounce "aïoli" (aye-OH-lee).

CROISSANT BURGERS WITH BASIL AÏOLI

PREP: 20 minutes / GRILL: 8 minutes / YIELD: 4 burgers

Sacré bleu! While using their national pastry as a burger bun might offend the French, one bite of this "Brie-tiful" take on the cheeseburger with a delicious garlicky kick just might change their minds.

1½	pounds ground beef chuck
½	pound ground pork
2	shallots, finely chopped
	Kosher salt or table salt and freshly ground black pepper, to taste
4	large croissants, sliced in half
½	cup mayonnaise
6	fresh basil leaves, finely chopped
1	tablespoon fresh lemon juice
2	cloves garlic, forced through a garlic press or finely chopped
8	ounces Brie, cut into 4 slices

1* Preheat a charcoal or gas grill to medium-high heat. In a large bowl combine the ground chuck, pork, shallot, salt, and pepper; mix well. Form into 4 oval patties to fit the croissants.

2* For the aïoli, combine the mayonnaise, basil leaves, lemon juice, and garlic.

3* Grill the burgers directly over medium-high heat until done (160°F), topping with the Brie when you flip them over. (Or cook the burgers indoors in a skillet or grill pan.) Toast the croissants while the burgers cook. Serve the burgers on the croissants; top with the aïoli.

(LESS) SLOPPY JANE

PREP: 15 minutes / COOK: 20 minutes / YIELD: 8 to 10 servings

My mom's sloppy joes were always a big family favorite. But the carnage I created devouring mine caused my mother and sister to cringe. Inspired by a touch of female sensibility, I developed this sandwich with a more delicate flavor and an open face that demands the daintiness of a knife and fork.

2 tablespoons olive oil
1 pound uncooked ground turkey
1 medium onion, finely chopped (½ cup)
1 red sweet pepper, finely chopped (¾ cup)
1 (15-ounce) can crushed tomatoes
1 tablespoon packed brown sugar
1 tablespoon Dijon-style mustard
1 tablespoon Worcestershire sauce
1 teaspoon bottled hot pepper sauce
Kosher salt or table salt and freshly ground black pepper, to taste
4 or 5 multigrain hamburger buns
Fresh chives

1* In a medium skillet heat the oil over high heat. Add the turkey; cook for 5 to 6 minutes or until browned and fully cooked, breaking up the turkey with a wooden spoon. Add the onion and sweet pepper; cook for 5 minutes more. Add the tomatoes, brown sugar, mustard, Worcestershire sauce, and hot pepper sauce; season with salt and pepper. Bring to a boil; lower the heat. Simmer for 10 minutes.

2* Toast the hamburger buns. Put a big spoonful of the meat mixture on each bun half. Garnish with snipped chives. Serve with a knife and fork.

Yeah, I know, the real name for a sloppy joe made from turkey is a sloppy tom. But this is my cookbook and I can call it whatever I want!

SHRIMP BURGERS WITH WASABI MAYO

PREP: 15 minutes / GRILL: 6 minutes / YIELD: 4 burgers or 14 mini burgers

When someone says "burger," most people think beef. But this blend of the bold richness of shrimp and the singular zing of wasabi takes the burger in a fresh new direction that even hard-core carnivores won't be able to resist!

½ cup mayonnaise
2 tablespoons prepared wasabi
    (available in the Asian section
    of your supermarket)
1 tablespoon soy sauce
½ teaspoon sugar
½ teaspoon grated fresh ginger
1 pound cooked peeled
    and deveined shrimp
1 egg
½ cup panko (Japanese-style
    bread crumbs)
¼ cup finely chopped fresh parsley
    Kosher salt or table salt and freshly
    ground black pepper, to taste
4 hamburger buns
    Tomato slices

1* Preheat a charcoal or gas grill to medium heat. For the wasabi mayo, in a small bowl stir together the mayonnaise, wasabi, soy sauce, sugar, and ginger. Cover and refrigerate until ready to use.

2* For the shrimp burgers, in a food processor place half of the shrimp and the egg; process until almost smooth. Coarsely chop the remaining shrimp and put it into a bowl. Add the processed shrimp and the panko, parsley, salt, and pepper. Form the mixture into 4 patties. Grill directly over medium heat about 3 to 4 minutes per side or until heated through. (Or fry in a skillet in a little oil.)

3* Place each burger on a bun. Top with a slice of tomato and some wasabi mayo. Cover with the bun top and serve.

FOR MINI BURGERS: Prepare the buns by using a 1½-inch diameter ring mold or biscuit cutter to cut out smaller buns. Form the shrimp mixture into patties, using a heaping tablespoon for each patty. Spray a large skillet with nonstick spray. Cook mini patties over medium heat for 3 to 4 minutes per side or until browned and heated through. Place a shrimp burger on a mini bun. Top with 1 to 2 slices of cherry tomato and some wasabi mayo. Cover with the bun top and secure with a cocktail pick. If desired, garnish with pickled cherry peppers, gherkins, olives, or jalapeño slices.

GEORGE'S SECRET ⌄

I didn't have a mold or biscuit cutter to cut the mini buns. Instead I used a clean glass to cut them to my desired size.

TERIYAKI PORTOBELLO BURGERS

PREP: 10 minutes / COOL: 30 minutes / MARINATE: 1 hour / GRILL: 6 minutes / YIELD: 4 servings

If you have a thing for the Asian essence of sweet teriyaki and the smoky, juicy punch of portobello mushrooms, then cover the page because you're about to start salivating. Top this burger with the kick of my wasabi slaw and you'll be watching the carnivores do their best vegetarian impersonation at your next barbecue.

¼ cup soy sauce
2 tablespoons balsamic vinegar
2 tablespoons sugar
1 clove garlic, forced through a
   garlic press or finely chopped
4 large portobello mushroom caps
2 cups shredded cabbage
3 tablespoons mayonnaise
1 tablespoon water
1 tablespoon soy sauce
1 teaspoon prepared wasabi
   (or more, if desired)
4 hamburger buns
   Teriyaki sauce (optional)

1 * In a small pan stir together the ½ cup soy sauce, vinegar, 1 tablespoon of the sugar, and the garlic. Cook over medium heat until the sugar melts. Cool for 30 minutes. Put the portobellos into a resealable plastic bag; add the cooled marinade. Seal the bag and marinate the mushrooms for 1 hour.

2 * For the slaw, put the cabbage in a large bowl. In a small bowl whisk together the mayonnaise, the remaining 1 tablespoon sugar, the water, the 1 tablespoon soy sauce, and the wasabi. Pour over the cabbage and toss well to coat.

3 * Preheat a charcoal or gas grill to medium heat. Grill the mushrooms directly over the heat for 3 to 4 minutes per side. (Or cook the portobellos in a grill pan or nonstick skillet.) Put the mushrooms on the buns and top each with ½ cup of the slaw. If desired, drizzle the serving platter lightly with teriyaki sauce and serve with additional prepared wasabi.

Useless Fact: Almost all sushi bars in the United States serve imitation wasabi made from horseradish, mustard seeds, and green food coloring. Sorry, the real stuff is just too expensive for riffraff like me and you!

BLT hot dog

PREP: 15 minutes / BAKE: 25 minutes / YIELD: 4 servings

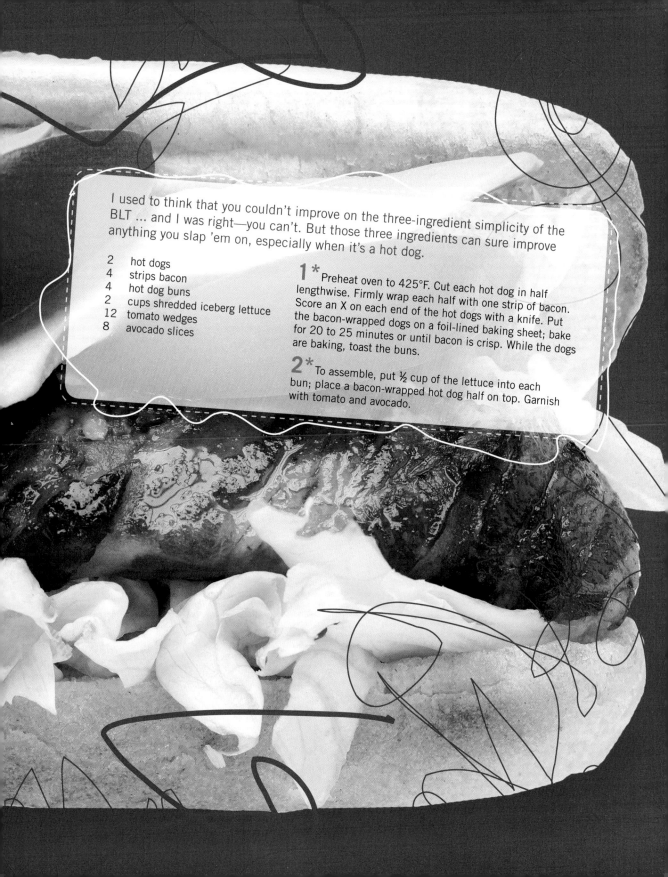

I used to think that you couldn't improve on the three-ingredient simplicity of the BLT ... and I was right—you can't. But those three ingredients can sure improve anything you slap 'em on, especially when it's a hot dog.

2   hot dogs
4   strips bacon
4   hot dog buns
2   cups shredded iceberg lettuce
12   tomato wedges
8   avocado slices

1 * Preheat oven to 425°F. Cut each hot dog in half lengthwise. Firmly wrap each half with one strip of bacon. Score an X on each end of the hot dogs with a knife. Put the bacon-wrapped dogs on a foil-lined baking sheet; bake for 20 to 25 minutes or until bacon is crisp. While the dogs are baking, toast the buns.

2 * To assemble, put ½ cup of the lettuce into each bun; place a bacon-wrapped hot dog half on top. Garnish with tomato and avocado.

VENEZUELAN HOT DOGS

PREP: 10 minutes / COOK: 5 minutes / YIELD: 4 servings

Growing up in Caracas, I inhaled countless numbers of Venezuela's unique interpretation of that most all-American of foods—the hot dog. Now you, too, can live the dream. Just make sure to include all the ingredients. Trust me, one bite and you'll wonder how you've lived this long without 'em!

8   hot dog rolls (preferably potato)
8   hot dogs (preferably pork)
1   sweet onion (such as Vidalia), cut up
¼   head cabbage
1   (6-ounce) bag potato chips
    Mayonnaise
    Mustard
    Ketchup

1* Fill a large pan fitted with a flat-bottomed steamer insert with water and bring to a boil. Arrange the rolls in the steamer and put the hot dogs in the boiling water. Put the steamer into the pan and cover. Cook about 5 minutes or until the hot dogs are heated through and the rolls are warm and soft. Be careful not to oversteam the rolls or they may become soggy.

2* While the dogs are cooking, put the onion into a food processor. Process with several on/off turns until finely chopped. Remove the onion to a bowl. Put the cabbage into the food processor; process with on/off turns until finely chopped. Finely crush the potato chips.

3* Put a hot dog in each bun and top with onion, cabbage, and crushed chips. Top with mayonnaise, mustard, and ketchup.

MILLION DOLLAR DOGS

PREP: 10 minutes / COOK: 5 minutes / YIELD: 4 servings

When I first concocted this hot dog, my friend Voreeg took one taste and proclaimed: "It tastes like a million dollars!" I'm hoping all of you will agree, and remember: I accept all major credit cards as payment!

4   all-beef franks
2   tablespoons mayonnaise
2   tablespoons ketchup
1   ripe avocado
1   tablespoon lime juice
½   cup snipped fresh cilantro
4   hot dog buns
    Potato chips

1* In a nonstick skillet cook the franks over medium-high heat for 4 to 5 minutes or until they are cooked through and crispy.

2* For the sauce, in a small bowl mix together the mayonnaise and ketchup. Dice the avocado, put it into another bowl, and toss with the lemon juice and cilantro. Toast the buns.

3* Place a frank in each bun, spread with 1 tablespoon of the sauce, and top with the avocado. Serve with potato chips.

George's Secret: It's easy staying green— sprinkle lime juice on avocados to prevent them from oxidizing and turning brown.

REUBEN MONTE CRISTO
SANDWICHES

PREP: 15 minutes / COOK: 4 minutes / YIELD: 2 sandwiches

Once again, the mad scientists at Short Attention Span Labs (okay, okay, the voices in my head!) have finally emerged from hours of painstaking experimentation to unveil a sandwich that merges two of my all-time favorites—the Reuben and Monte Cristo—into one mouthwatering Frankenstein-ian feast!

4 slices rye bread
⅓ cup Thousand Island salad dressing
10 thin slices corned beef
6 slices Swiss cheese
1 cup drained sauerkraut
2 eggs
¼ cup milk
1 tablespoon paprika
2 tablespoons butter
   Thousand Island salad dressing (optional)

1* Spread each bread slice evenly with salad dressing. Arrange half of the corned beef slices on one piece of bread; top it with half of the cheese slices. Cover with half of the sauerkraut and another slice of bread, dressing side down. Repeat to make the second sandwich.

2* In a shallow dish beat together the eggs, milk, and paprika. Gently dip each sandwich into the egg mixture, pressing lightly so the bread absorbs the liquid.

3* Heat the butter in a nonstick skillet over medium-low heat. Add the sandwiches. Cover and cook for 2 to 3 minutes or until the bottom is browned and the cheese starts to melt. Flip the sandwiches, cover, and cook for 2 to 3 minutes more. If desired, serve with additional Thousand Island dressing.

George's Secret: Take this sandwich to the next level of decadence by whipping up some homemade Thousand Island dressing: Mix 1 cup mayo, ½ cup ketchup, 3 tablespoons pickle relish, and one chopped, peeled hard-cooked egg. Shhhh . . . just don't tell the fast food joints you know what's in their "secret sauce."

CUBAN SANDWICH CASSEROLE

PREP: 15 minutes / CHILL: overnight: / BAKE: 1 hour / STAND: 10 minutes / YIELD: 6 to 8 servings

How on earth do you serve a pressed sandwich to a bunch of your closest friends for dinner? Unless you own a dry cleaner's giant trouser press, you're going to need to try it my way. This will allow you to pack all that authentic Cuban flavor into one of my favorite culinary forms—the casserole!

1	tablespoon butter
16	slices sandwich bread
10 to 12	slices Swiss cheese
10 to 12	slices baked ham
3	dill pickles, thinly sliced
6	eggs
3	cups milk
2	teaspoons dry mustard
3	cups cornflakes, crushed
½	cup butter (1 stick), melted

1* One day ahead grease a 13×9×2-inch baking pan with 1 tablespoon butter. Trim the crusts off the bread and line the bottom of the pan with 8 slices. Place half of the cheese slices over the bread. Layer all of the ham over the cheese. Add the remaining cheese slices, the pickle slices, and the remaining bread. In a bowl whisk together the eggs, milk, and dry mustard. Pour the egg mixture over the casserole, cover with plastic wrap, and refrigerate overnight.

2* Remove the casserole from the refrigerator 30 minutes before baking. Preheat the oven to 350°F. Stir together the cornflakes and melted butter. Spread the cereal mix evenly over the casserole. Bake for 1 hour or until puffy and browned around the edges. Let stand for 10 minutes before serving.

SO THAT'S HOW YOU DO IT ⌄

Use a channel tool (the wide channeling blade often found on citrus zesters) to cut vertical strips off the pickle. The slices look like flowers!

BREADLESS TUNA MELT

PREP: 15 minutes / BROIL: 3 minutes / YIELD: 2 servings

Though I unabashedly worship all things bready, I am sympathetic to the needs of my carb-o-phobic brothers and sisters. This spectacular open-faced sandwich with fresh, flavorful tomato in place of bread is my gift to them.

1   large beefsteak tomato
1   cup prepared tuna salad or
      George's Artichoke Tuna Salad
      (page 50)
     Chipotle-flavored bottled
      hot pepper sauce
2   slices pepper Jack cheese
     Chopped fresh cilantro (optional)

1* Preheat the broiler. Bring a small pan of water to a boil. Fill a small bowl with cold water and ice cubes. Remove the tomato stem and score an X in the bottom of the tomato. Gently lower the tomato into the boiling water for 5 to 10 seconds or until the skin starts to peel. Immediately remove the tomato and submerge it in the cold water. Slip the skin off; pat dry with paper towels.

2* Cut the top and bottom off the tomato, then cut it in half horizontally. Place ½ cup of tuna salad on each tomato half. Add hot pepper sauce to taste and top each stack with 1 slice of cheese.

3* Place tomato stacks on a broiler pan. Broil the tomato stacks until the cheese is melted and bubbling. If desired, sprinkle with chopped cilantro. Serve immediately.

HOLY GRAIL OF OPTIONS ⌄

YELLOW   PLUM

CHERRY

Use yellow, plum, or cherry tomatoes to turn this recipe into an hors d'oeuvre. Cut slices of plum tomatoes to serve as crostini. Or hollow out cherry tomatoes; fill with tuna and cheese.

APRICOT AND BRIE GRILLED SANDWICH

PREP: 5 minutes / COOK: 6 minutes / YIELD: 1 sandwich

In *Ham on the Street*, I once proclaimed that a combination of any bread, cheese, and preserves yields an eye-opening, lip-smacking twist on the classic grilled cheese. And I was right. This one is my all-time favorite (so far!).

Butter, softened
2   thick slices challah
    or other egg bread
3   thick slices Brie cheese
1   tablespoon pine nuts
2   tablespoons apricot preserves

1 * Lightly butter one side of the bread slices. Place 1 piece, butter side down, in a nonstick skillet over low heat; top with the slices of Brie. Carefully sprinkle the pine nuts on the Brie. Spread the unbuttered side of the other piece of bread with apricot preserves and put it, preserves side down, on the cheese. Cook about 3 minutes or until browned; flip the sandwich and cook about 3 minutes more or until the second side has browned. Serve warm.

HOLY GRAIL OF OPTIONS

GOAT CHEESE & STRAWBERRY JELLY

CHEDDAR CHEESE & BLACKBERRY JAM

GORGONZOLA & PEPPER JELLY

Try one of these options for your grilled sandwich: goat cheese and strawberry jelly, Gorgonzola and pepper jelly, or cheddar cheese and blackberry jam.

LET

GET

COM

HUNGRY
FOR SOME
HOMESTYLE
COOKIN'?

NOTHING SAYS COMFORT COOKING
BETTER THAN A CASSEROLE. I HAVE
SOME THAT ARE THE CULINARY
EQUIVALENT OF GRANDPA'S LA-Z-BOY!
PLUS A FEW CLASSICS REIMAGINED
WITH A DASH OF DURAN!

S

MFY

THE CHICKEN-FRIED JEEP

Over the years, I've had the opportunity to live, work, and travel all over the world. I've studied classic French cuisine and sampled ethnic specialties. I consider myself an adventurous eater with a palate that's ready for anything. **But if I had to choose whatever I wanted for one last meal, there's no doubt in my mind what that meal would be: FRIED CHICKEN.**

I've had many, MANY fried chicken meals, and thankfully none of them has been my last (though I did get food poisoning from the drumstick special at Uncle Ralph's House of Fried Meals somewhere in West Texas!). Out of the many fantastic chicken meals, I have no problem selecting the most memorable.

It came as I prepared to depart for culinary school in Paris. I had some friends help me pack up my Manhattan apartment and haul everything out to a storage locker in New Jersey. To thank them, I decided to forgo the traditional postmove meal of pizza and beer for something more meaningful: fried chicken and beer!

I loaded my car with a feast's worth of fried chicken takeout and headed for a friend's house to celebrate. The beer was cold, the chicken was hot, and everyone was having a great time. Then my cell phone rang. It was a guy calling about my car. I had placed an ad, hoping to sell it before I left, but hadn't had much interest. Until now. "C'mon over!" I said, happily gnawing on a wing.

I met my prospective buyer outside and we took the car for a quick spin. We hadn't gone more than two blocks when he turned to me, confused, and said: **"Okay, is this car deep-fried?" Seems my chicken feast had literally soaked into the Jeep's upholstery.** I smiled weakly and said, "Make me an offer?" He did, and I took it—for a thousand dollars less than I was asking. It was the most expensive fried chicken meal I'd ever had.

GUILTLESS OVEN-FRIED CHICKEN

PREP: 10 minutes / BAKE: 20 minutes / YIELD: 4 servings

Yeah, I love deep-fried chicken as much as the next heart patient. But
I guarantee that my no-guilt version will get you off the grease for good.
Prepare to kick the bucket (of chicken, that is)!

1 cup low-fat mayonnaise
1 tablespoon garlic powder
1 tablespoon paprika
1 teaspoon chili powder
3 tablespoons water
  Kosher salt or table salt and freshly
    ground black pepper, to taste
4 chicken thighs, skin removed
  Nonstick cooking spray
2 cups panko (Japanese-style
    bread crumbs)

1* Preheat the oven to 350°F. In a large bowl combine the
mayonnaise, garlic powder, paprika, and chili powder. Mix with water,
1 tablespoon at a time, to make it the consistency of whipping cream;
season with salt and pepper. Add the chicken pieces; coat well with
the mayonnaise mixture.

2* Lightly coat a nonstick baking sheet with cooking spray. Pour
the panko onto a plate. Toss the chicken thighs, one at a time, in the
crumbs to completely coat. Place the chicken on the baking sheet;
coat with cooking spray. Bake for 20 to 25 minutes or until the
chicken is browned and cooked through, turning once.

HOLY GRAIL OF OPTIONS ⌄

MILD CURRY

GREEN CURRY

RED CURRY

For a more
fragrant version
of this recipe,
mix some curry
paste with the
mayo instead
of the spices.

STUFFED BUFFALO WING

PREP: 10 minutes / COOK: 7 minutes / BAKE: 8 minutes / YIELD: 4 servings **CHICKEN BREASTS**

If you're looking for love and you love buffalo wings, your prayers have been answered! I've transformed one of the world's messiest meals into a decadent dish that can actually be served on a date.

4 skinless, boneless
chicken breast halves
4 ounces blue cheese
Kosher salt or table salt and
freshly ground black pepper
2 tablespoons olive oil
½ cup (1 stick) butter
2 tablespoons white vinegar
2 tablespoons bottled hot sauce
Crumbled blue cheese (optional)
Thin celery stalks (optional)

1* Preheat the oven to 350°F. Using a sharp knife, cut a pocket in each chicken breast. Stuff one-fourth of the blue cheese into each breast. Secure the openings with toothpicks and season the chicken with salt and pepper.

2* In an ovenproof nonstick skillet heat the oil over medium heat. Add the chicken and cook for 3 to 4 minutes per side or until browned. Transfer the chicken to oven; bake for 8 to 10 minutes or until no longer pink (170°F). Return chicken to stovetop.

3* In a small pan combine the butter, vinegar, and hot sauce. Cook over medium heat until bubbling. Pour half the sauce over the hot chicken; cook over medium heat for 1 minute. Remove the toothpicks. Serve the chicken with the remaining sauce. If desired, sprinkle with crumbled blue cheese and garnish with celery.

MYSTERY THINGAMAJIGS ⌄

One of the reasons we should all be glad we live in the 21st century: reusable heatproof silicone twine to hold stuffed chicken breasts together! Just tuck the loose ends into the loop to avoid burns.

COQ AU COLA

PREP: 20 minutes / COOK: 1 hour 15 minutes / YIELD: 6 servings

When I first conceived this recipe, all I had was the name and a dream. Now that dream is reality, as I've given the quintessential French fricassee an all-American update.

¼ cup all-purpose flour
1 teaspoon kosher salt or
   ¾ teaspoon table salt
¼ teaspoon freshly ground black pepper
6 chicken thighs, skin removed
2 tablespoons vegetable oil
4 to 6 slices bacon, chopped
2 medium onions, finely
   chopped (1 cup)
3 carrots, peeled and sliced (1½ cups)
1 (8-ounce) package button
   mushrooms, sliced
3 cloves garlic, finely chopped
1 cup cola
1 (14.5-ounce) can diced tomatoes
1 tablespoon snipped fresh thyme
Mashed potatoes

1 * In a shallow bowl mix together the flour, salt, and pepper. Dredge the chicken thighs in the flour mixture.

2 * In a heavy skillet heat the oil over medium-high heat. Add the chicken thighs and cook for 3 to 4 minutes on each side. Remove the chicken and set aside. Add the bacon to the skillet and cook about 1 minute. Add the onion, carrot, mushrooms, and garlic; cook for 4 to 5 minutes or until the onions soften. Return the chicken to the pan. Add the cola, tomatoes, and thyme. Partially cover the skillet and bring to a boil. Reduce the heat to a simmer. Cover and cook about 1 hour or until the juices thicken and the chicken is no longer pink (170°F), stirring every 15 minutes. Serve with mashed potatoes.

MYSTERY THINGAMAJIGS ⌄

Finding a place to rest the spoon while making a stew usually results in a puddle of gravy on the counter. This gadget solves the problem by allowing you to rest your spoon on the side of your skillet or pot. See ya, drips!

MICROWAVE CHICKEN CURRY

PREP: 10 minutes / COOK: 15 minutes / STAND: 3 minutes / YIELD: 4 servings

Used to be, if someone said he or she cooked your chicken in the microwave it was your cue to leave. But this moist, Indian-inspired dish will not only keep people in their seats, they'll demand seconds!

3   tablespoons olive oil
2   tablespoons Indian curry paste
4   skinless, boneless chicken breasts,
        cut into strips
2   (13.5-ounce) cans unsweetened
        coconut milk
2   tablespoons soy sauce
½   bunch fresh basil, snipped
        (about ¼ cup)
½   bunch fresh cilantro, snipped
        (about ¼ cup)
      Kosher salt or table salt and freshly
        ground black pepper, to taste
      Hot steamed rice
      Paprika
1   green onion, thinly sliced
      Crushed pink peppercorns (optional)

1* In a large microwave-safe dish with a cover mix together the oil and curry paste. Microwave on high (100% power) for 3 minutes. Stir in the chicken; cover and microwave on medium (50% power) for 8 minutes.

2* Stir in the coconut milk, soy sauce, basil, and cilantro; season with salt and pepper. Cover and microwave on medium for 4 minutes. Stir the mixture again, cover, and let stand for 3 or 4 minutes. Serve over rice and garnish with paprika and green onion. If desired, sprinkle with crushed peppercorns.

George's Secret: Not all microwaves are created equal! The wattage on microwaves ranges from 400 watts to 1,500 watts. This recipe was created using an 1,100-watt microwave, so adjust your time accordingly.

stuffed lasagna rolls

PREP: 25 minutes / COOK: 7 minutes
BAKE: 20 minutes / YIELD: 5 to 6 servings

Many of us struggle with life's conundrums. Why are we here? Is this all there is? What do you do with the six sheets of lasagna pasta that are left over in your pantry? You're on your own with the first two, but I have the perfect solution for number three: Make some stuffed lasagna rolls!

12 no-cook lasagna noodles
2 to 3 hot Italian sausages
1½ cups part-skim ricotta cheese
1 cup grated Parmesan cheese
1 egg, beaten
½ cup chopped fresh basil
1 teaspoon kosher salt or
    ¾ teaspoon table salt
1 teaspoon freshly ground
    black pepper
1 (28-ounce) can
    crushed tomatoes
1 cup shredded
    mozzarella cheese

1* In a large pan of boiling, salted water cook the lasagna noodles for 2 to 3 minutes or until they are just soft (don't overcook them). Drain and rinse with cold water. Drain on paper towels.

2* Remove the casings from the sausages. Crumble the meat into a nonstick skillet. Cook over high heat about 5 to 6 minutes or until browned, breaking up the sausage with a wooden spoon. Remove from the pan and set aside. In a bowl mix the ricotta, Parmesan, egg, basil, salt, and pepper until combined. Set aside. Preheat the oven to 350°F. In a 13×9×2-inch lasagna pan evenly spread half of the tomatoes.

3* To assemble the lasagna rolls, place a lasagna noodle on a work surface with the short side toward you. Put 2 tablespoons of the ricotta mixture on the bottom half of the noodle; add 1 tablespoon of the cooked sausage. Roll noodle starting at the bottom and place in the lasagna pan. Prepare the remaining noodles in the same way, lining them up in the pan. Spread the remaining tomatoes over the rolls and top with the mozzarella cheese. Cover with foil and bake for 10 to 15 minutes more. Uncover and bake for 10 to 15 minutes or until the cheese is bubbling and lightly browned.

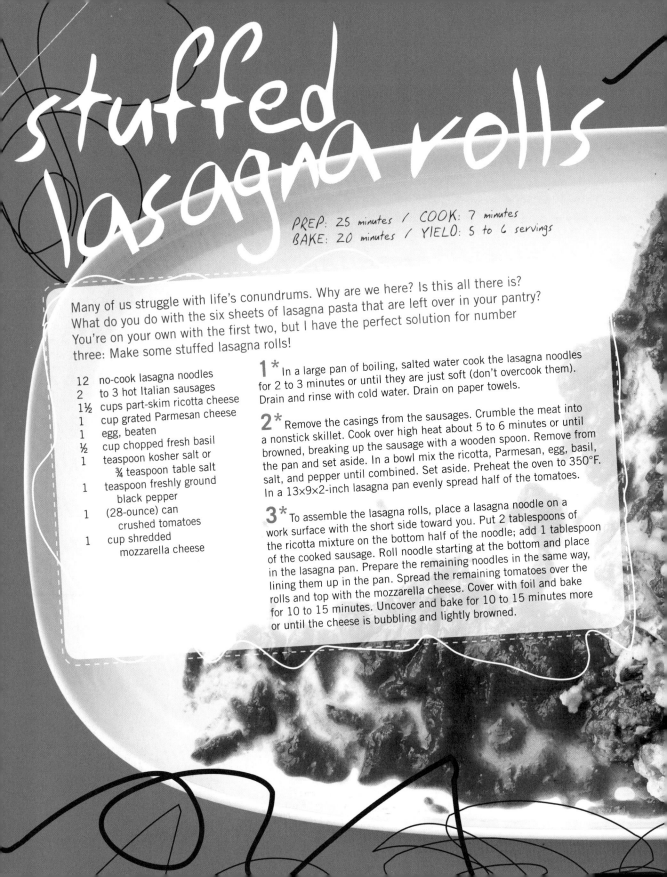

TEX-MEX LASAGNA

PREP: 25 minutes / COOK: 15 minutes / BAKE: 30 minutes / STAND: 10 minutes / YIELD: 4 to 6 servings

It may hail from Italy, but believe me, lasagna can travel. With some flour tortillas layered with a butt-kicking filling, this "Texican" version makes for one delectable dish. You can vary the heat level by the salsa you choose—I like it hot!

2 tablespoons olive oil
1 large onion, chopped (1 cup)
1 tablespoon taco seasoning
½ cup chicken stock or broth
1 deli roasted chicken, skin and
    bones removed and shredded
1 (16-ounce) jar salsa
1 (10.75-ounce) can cream
    of mushroom soup
2 cups shredded Tex-Mex
    cheese blend (8 ounces)
1 cup fresh cilantro, snipped
    Nonstick cooking spray
6 (9-inch) flour tortillas
1 cup tortilla chips, crushed
1 cup shredded cheddar cheese

1 * Preheat the oven to 350°F. In a large skillet heat the oil over medium-high heat. Add the onion and cook for 5 to 6 minutes or until soft and translucent. Stir in the taco seasoning. Add the chicken broth; bring to a boil. Add the shredded chicken. Reduce the heat to low and simmer for 5 minutes. Stir in the salsa, soup, Tex-Mex cheese, and cilantro. Simmer for 2 to 3 minutes more.

2 * Coat a 9×9×2-inch baking pan or other 2-quart casserole dish with nonstick cooking spray. Place 2 tortillas in the bottom of the pan, folding over the sides of the tortillas to fit. Spoon half the chicken mixture over the tortillas. Repeat layers once more; top with the remaining 2 tortillas. Mix crushed chips with cheddar cheese; sprinkle over the top. Bake about 30 minutes or until the lasagna is bubbling and lightly browned. Let stand for 10 minutes before serving.

Useless Fact: The term Tex-Mex was first used as a nickname for the Texas-Mexican Railway in 1875.

PENNE TUNA CASSEROLE

PREP: 10 minutes / COOK: 15 minutes / BAKE: 30 minutes / STAND: 10 minutes / YIELD: 6 to 8 servings

This potluck comfort classic is so good, you may decide not to share it! Then again, after the tenth day of leftovers, maybe you will.

Nonstick cooking spray
1 pound dried penne pasta
Kosher salt or table salt
4 tablespoons (½ stick) butter
4 tablespoons all-purpose flour
1 quart milk (4 cups)
2 tablespoons snipped fresh thyme or 2 teaspoons dried thyme, crushed
1 teaspoon cayenne pepper
2 (6-ounce) cans water-pack tuna, drained
1 (10-ounce) package frozen peas
¼ cup fresh lemon juice
¾ cup dry bread crumbs
¼ cup grated Parmesan cheese
3 tablespoons butter, melted

1 * Preheat the oven to 350°F. Coat a 13×9×2-inch baking pan or a large ovenproof casserole with nonstick cooking spray.

2 * Cook the pasta in plenty of boiling salted water for 8 to 10 minutes or until it is almost tender. (The pasta will absorb the liquid from the sauce as it finishes cooking in the oven.) Drain, rinse with cold water; drain and set aside.

3 * In a large pan melt the 4 tablespoons butter over medium heat. Add the flour and whisk to combine. Whisk constantly about 2 minutes or until the flour is cooked but not brown. Remove from heat. Slowly add the milk, whisking to prevent lumps. Cook about 8 to 10 minutes or until the mixture thickens, stirring frequently. Stir in the thyme and cayenne pepper. Stir in the pasta, tuna, peas, and lemon juice. Pour into the prepared pan.

4 * Combine the bread crumbs, Parmesan, and melted butter. Spoon the topping evenly over the casserole. Bake about 30 minutes or until the top is golden brown and the mixture is bubbling. Let stand for 10 minutes before serving.

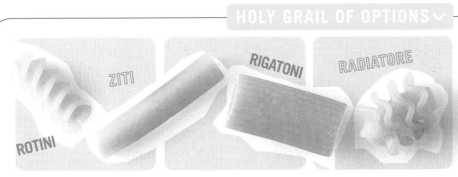

HOLY GRAIL OF OPTIONS ⌄

ZITI

RIGATONI

RADIATORE

ROTINI

Feel free to replace the penne with the pasta of your choice. Some of my favorites are shown here.

PIZZA FONDUE

PREP: 15 minutes / COOK: 20 minutes / YIELD: 6 to 8 servings

My quest to reimagine pizza in every possible form continues. Here the humble slice is deconstructed into a bite-size, decadently delicious, dippable treat.

2 tablespoons butter
¼ cup finely chopped onion
2 cloves garlic, forced through a
   garlic press or finely chopped
1 tomato, seeded and diced
1 tablespoon dried basil, crushed
1 tablespoon dried oregano, crushed
⅛ teaspoon crushed red pepper
   Kosher salt or table salt and freshly
   ground black pepper, to taste
6 ounces dry white wine
2 cups shredded mozzarella
   cheese (8 ounces)
2 cups shredded cheddar
   cheese (8 ounces)
   Assorted dippers (such as button
   mushrooms, broccoli florets,
   cubed ham, sweet pepper strips,
   and pepperoni)

1* In a medium pan melt the butter over medium heat. Add the onion and garlic; cook for 6 to 8 minutes or until lightly browned. Add the tomato, basil, oregano, crushed red pepper, salt, and pepper; simmer for 5 minutes. Add the wine; return to a simmer. Add the cheeses; stir until completely melted. Serve in a fondue pot or double boiler with the assorted dippers.

HOLY GRAIL OF OPTIONS ⌄

BOBOLI PIZZA SHELL

PICKLED PEPPERS

MEATBALLS

There are endless dipping options for this cheesy delight. Also try Boboli pizza shell pieces or breadsticks, meatballs, pickled peppers, and/or cubed turkey.

caramelized onion & blue cheese pizza

PREP: 15 minutes / COOK: 20 minutes
BAKE: 10 minutes / YIELD: 8 servings

Caramelized onions are one of my favorite ways to give a recipe a high-end flourish. The key is to cook the onions slowly to release their natural sugars.

2   pounds onions, sliced
2   tablespoons olive oil
     Dash sugar
½   cup tomato sauce
2   prepared pizza crusts
1   cup shredded mozzarella cheese
      (4 ounces)
8   ounces blue cheese, crumbled
      (2 cups)

1* In a skillet cook the onions, olive oil, and sugar over medium heat for 20 to 25 minutes or until the onions are tender and brown, stirring frequently. Reduce the heat if the onions are browning too quickly. Set aside.

2* Preheat the oven to 450°F. Spread half the tomato sauce over one of the crusts. Top with half the caramelized onions and half the mozzarella cheese. Repeat with the other crust. Bake for 10 to 15 minutes or until the cheese is browned and bubbling. Remove from the oven and sprinkle with the blue cheese.

ARMENIAN PIZZA

PREP: 15 minutes / BAKE: 8 minutes / YIELD: 4 servings

Also known as *lahmajoon,* this thin, crispy treat will fill your kitchen with the mouthwatering Armenian aromas I grew up loving. This pizza is a tasty alternative to the Italian classic.

2   cloves garlic
1   medium onion, coarsely
      chopped (½ cup)
1   small green sweet pepper,
      seeded and coarsely chopped
1   pound ground lamb
1   (14.5-ounce) can diced tomatoes
1   (6-ounce) can tomato paste
¼   cup snipped fresh parsley
½   teaspoon ground cumin
½   teaspoon cayenne pepper
    Kosher salt or table salt and
      freshly ground black pepper
4   flour tortillas
    Fresh snipped parsley
    Lemon wedges

1 * Preheat the oven to 400°F. Pulse the garlic in a food processor until minced. Add the onion and pulse until chopped. Add the sweet pepper and pulse until chopped. Add the lamb, tomatoes, tomato paste, parsley, cumin, cayenne, salt, and black pepper. Process until the mixture is the consistency of hummus.

2 * Spread a thin layer of the meat mixture all the way to the edge of each tortilla. Bake directly on the oven rack for 8 to 10 minutes or until the edges are browned and the meat is cooked through. If the tortilla begins to inflate in the oven, pierce the top with a fork. To serve, squeeze some lemon over the top. If desired, garnish with fresh parsley. Fold the pizza into quarters, and eat it out of hand.

HOLY GRAIL OF OPTIONS ⌄

GROUND TURKEY

GROUND CHICKEN

GROUND BEEF

Since Americans consume only about 0.8 pound of lamb per year, I'm guessing you're gonna want to try this recipe with other meats such as ground turkey, chicken, or beef.

BALSAMIC ROASTED BRUSSELS SPROUTS

PREP: 20 minutes / BAKE: 50 minutes / YIELD: 6 to 8 servings

Though they probably can't top the lima bean on most people's loathe-o-meter, Brussels sprouts inspire plenty of disdain. That, however, is about to change. I guarantee that one taste of this robust recipe will turn even the staunchest sprout slagger into a sprout booster. If I'm wrong, I'll reimburse you for the sprouts!

2 pounds Brussels sprouts
1 (1-pound) bag frozen pearl onions
4 medium carrots, sliced (4 cups)
8 slices bacon, coarsely chopped
¼ cup pine nuts
1 tablespoon snipped fresh thyme or 1 teaspoon dried thyme, crushed
1 tablespoon snipped fresh oregano or 1 teaspoon dried oregano, crushed
½ teaspoon kosher salt or ¼ teaspoon table salt
¼ teaspoon freshly ground black pepper
½ cup extra virgin olive oil
⅓ cup balsamic vinegar

1* Preheat the oven to 400°F. Cut off the bottoms of the sprouts and trim off any damaged outer leaves. Soak the sprouts in a bowl of cold water for a few minutes; drain well. Cut the sprouts in half and put them in a large bowl. Add the onions, carrot, bacon, pine nuts, thyme, oregano, salt, and pepper. Add the oil and vinegar; toss well to coat.

2* Place the mixture in a roasting pan; bake for 25 minutes. Stir and bake for 25 minutes more or until the Brussels sprouts are nicely browned and vinegar has caramelized. Serve immediately.

Useless Fact: Ever wonder why these guys look like mini cabbages? Because they're family! Feel free to replace the sprouts with coarsely chopped cabbage for a less crunchy version.

BACON CREAMED SPINACH

PREP: 10 minutes / COOK: 20 minutes / YIELD: 4 to 6 servings

For me, the decadent richness of creamed spinach is the perfect accompaniment to a nice thick steak. Well, almost perfect. Once again the answer to the eternal question "Would it be better with some bacon?" is a resounding YES!

6   slices bacon
1   medium onion, chopped (½ cup)
2   (10-ounce) packages frozen chopped
      spinach, thawed and drained
1   cup milk
2   tablespoons butter
2   tablespoons all-purpose flour
½   cup dairy sour cream
      Kosher salt or table salt and freshly
      ground black pepper, to taste

1 * In a nonstick skillet fry the bacon over medium-low heat for 6 to 8 minutes or until crisp. Drain on paper towels. Add the onion to the skillet and cook for 5 to 6 minutes or until it is soft and translucent. Add the spinach and cook for 2 minutes more.

2 * Warm the milk in a small pan or in the microwave. In a 1-quart saucepan melt the butter over medium-low heat. Whisk in the flour and cook for 1 minute. Add the warm milk, whisking constantly, and cook for 5 to 6 minutes or until it thickens. Pour the white sauce over the spinach and onion and cook for 2 minutes. Remove from the heat and stir in the sour cream. Crumble in the bacon and adjust the seasoning with salt and pepper. Serve immediately.

Frying bacon smells great but can make a big mess. Try the crispy oven method: Place the slices on parchment paper on a baking sheet. Bake at 350°F for 12 to 15 minutes.

ROSEMARY-GARLIC MASHED POTATOES

PREP: 15 minutes / COOK: 20 minutes / ROAST: 45 minutes / YIELD: 8 to 10 servings

This delectable side dish is named after my third-grade crush, Rosemary Garlic. Okay, that's a complete fabrication. Seriously, this recipe gets its name from the pungent punch of rosemary and the savory sweetness of slow-roasted garlic, which inject the plain ol' potato with unforgettable flavor.

1   bulb garlic
1½   teaspoons extra virgin olive oil
3   pounds russet potatoes,
      peeled and cubed
      Kosher salt or table salt
1½   cups whipping cream
3   sprigs fresh rosemary
½   cup butter (1 stick),
      at room temperature
      Freshly ground black pepper
      Snipped fresh rosemary (optional)

1* Preheat the oven to 400°F. Cut the top off the garlic; wrap the bulb in foil, leaving the top cut edge exposed. Drizzle with the olive oil. Roast for 45 minutes or until the garlic is soft and caramelized. Set aside to cool.

2* Meanwhile, in a medium pan cover the potatoes with water and add a big pinch of salt. Bring to a boil over high heat. Lower the heat to medium and simmer about 20 minutes or until the potatoes are tender; drain well.

3* While the potatoes are cooking, warm the cream and rosemary in a small pan over low heat. Strain out the rosemary.

4* Put the hot potatoes through a ricer into a large bowl. Squeeze in the roasted garlic and add some of the warm cream. Mix well. Add the butter; mix again. Add more cream if necessary. Season with salt and pepper. If desired, garnish with snipped rosemary. Serve immediately.

George's Secret: So what are the best potatoes for mashing? Personally I like Yukon golds or russets because they easily absorb liquids and flavors, making for richer, tastier spuds.

GO YUKON!

RUSSETS #1

SAY NO TO FINGERLING!

CORN BREAD MUFFIN STUFFING

PREP: 15 minutes / COOK: 15 minutes / BAKE: 45 minutes / YIELD: 8 to 10 servings

There are lots of ways to stuff a turkey, and I love just about all of them. But there's something about the sweetness of the corn muffins that makes this recipe one that I turn to any time of year.

2   tablespoons extra virgin olive oil
2   (4-ounce) hot Italian sausages, casings removed
1   cup chopped carrot
1   cup chopped celery (2 stalks)
1   cup chopped onion (1 large)
    Kosher salt or table salt and freshly ground black pepper
½   cup snipped fresh sage
4   (4-ounce) corn muffins
3   eggs
½   cup chicken stock or broth
    Nonstick cooking spray

1 * Heat the oven to 350°F. In a skillet heat 1 tablespoon of the oil over medium-high heat. Add the sausage; cook about 5 minutes or until browned and cooked through, breaking the meat into small pieces with a wooden spoon. Drain on a plate lined with paper towels; set aside to cool. Wipe excess fat from the pan with paper towels.

2 * In the same skillet heat the remaining 1 tablespoon oil over medium-high heat. Add the carrot, celery, and onion. Season with salt and pepper; add the sage. Cook about 10 minutes or until the vegetables are soft. Set aside.

3 * Crumble the corn muffins into a large bowl. Add the cooled sausage and the vegetables. Add the eggs and ¼ cup of the chicken stock. Using your hands, mix well, adding more stock if the stuffing is too dry. Coat a 2-quart ovenproof baking dish with nonstick cooking spray. Put the stuffing in the dish and bake for 45 minutes to 1 hour or until the top is browned and crispy.

GEORGE'S SECRET ⌄

Go that extra mile (or 15 minutes) and make a batch of instant mix corn bread instead of using purchased muffins. It's less sweet than corn bread muffins and allows the sausage flavor to be more dominant.

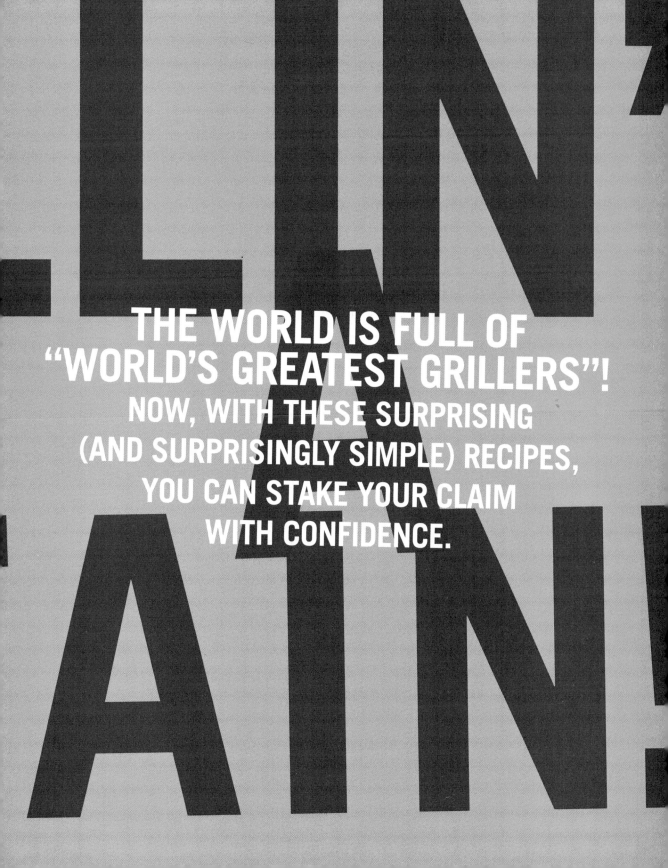

THE WORLD IS FULL OF "WORLD'S GREATEST GRILLERS"! NOW, WITH THESE SURPRISING (AND SURPRISINGLY SIMPLE) RECIPES, YOU CAN STAKE YOUR CLAIM WITH CONFIDENCE.

WORTH A VISIT FROM THE NYFO

Being of Armenian extraction, I consider my possession of the "grilling gene" practically a birthright. **But grilling can be a problem for those of us who call an apartment building home. Luckily I don't let anything— or anyone—stop me from grilling.**

• Not my Parisian landlady, who warned me over and over to cease my regular rooftop barbecues (which made me, the "crazy American with the rooftop grill," something of a neighborhood celebrity/curiosity) until she finally had to evict me.

• Not my Brooklyn landlord, who had to read me the riot act after receiving one too many complaints about "warm, savory raindrops" falling on pedestrians as I kebab-ed up a storm on my tiny terrace.

• Not even the fire department! Okay, well, the fire department can stop me . . . and they did. You see, I was living in my first Manhattan apartment, which had no outdoor space. At this time, I was in the midst of my infamous "ribs period" and was elated to find an indoor oven smoker! I got the thing home, loaded up the wood chips, applied the rub to my ribs, and commenced smokin'.

Within minutes my tiny apartment was filled with smoke. But thanks to some rapid-fire window-opening (and frantic fan-turning-on-ing), I was able to ventilate the premises. Or so I thought, until I heard sirens and looked out the window to find several fire trucks below. **I heard loud banging on the doors up and down my hallway. I opened up to see several New York City firefighters in hot pursuit of a fire!**

With my apartment door open, there was no denying the smoky aroma was mine. I fessed up to my transgression and promised to never, ever use my indoor smoker again. I offered to share my ribs with the firefighters, but they got called away before I could fix them a plate. Their loss, because those ribs were delicious!

ROSEMARY-LEMON BABY BACK RIBS

PREP: 5 minutes / MARINATE: overnight / GRILL: 45 minutes / YIELD: 4 servings

When it comes to ribs, I prefer to gnaw. But with a little extra cooking time, this fantastic flavor combo will easily satisfy any member of the "fall off the bone" club.

2   pounds pork baby back ribs
1   tablespoon dried rosemary, crushed
1   tablespoon dried oregano, crushed
2   teaspoons shredded lemon zest
1   teaspoon paprika
1   teaspoon onion powder
1   teaspoon garlic powder
1   teaspoon ground cinnamon
1   teaspoon kosher salt or
     ¾ teaspoon table salt
½   teaspoon freshly ground black pepper
½   cup fresh lemon juice
½   cup honey
     Nonstick cooking spray

1* Remove the membrane from the back of the ribs or ask your butcher to do it. In a small bowl combine the rosemary, oregano, lemon zest, paprika, onion powder, garlic powder, cinnamon, salt, and pepper. Put the ribs on a platter; rub the dry mix into both sides. Cover and refrigerate overnight.

2* Remove the ribs from the refrigerator while you heat a charcoal or gas grill to medium heat. For the mop sauce, mix together the lemon juice and honey; set aside. Spray both sides of the ribs with nonstick cooking spray. Grill the ribs, bone side down, directly over medium heat for 20 minutes. Flip the ribs over and cook for 10 minutes more. Flip again to the bone side and cook 15 minutes more, basting with the mop sauce every 5 minutes.

Useless Fact: A little "hog-geography": Baby back ribs are from the upper back loin of the pig. They're the most popular and expensive ribs . . . and worth every penny!

SPICE-RUBBED BEER CAN CHICKEN

PREP: 15 minutes / GRILL: 1 hour / YIELD: 4 servings

Maybe it's just me, but when I see a chicken standing upright and begging to be eaten, I can't help but comply! Caution: Don't drink the leftover beer!

½ cup extra virgin olive oil
2 tablespoons garlic powder
1 tablespoon ground cumin
1 tablespoon ground coriander
1 tablespoon paprika
1 tablespoon kosher salt or 2 teaspoons table salt
1 tablespoon freshly ground black pepper
1 teaspoon cayenne pepper
1 (3½- to 4-pound) chicken
1 (12-ounce) can beer

1 * Preheat a charcoal or gas grill with a cover (be sure the cover is high enough to accommodate the bird) to medium heat. Put a drip pan below the center of the grill rack.

2 * Stir together the olive oil, garlic powder, cumin, coriander, paprika, salt, black pepper, and cayenne pepper. (This mixture will keep, covered, in the refrigerator for 1 week.) Rub it all over the chicken, inside and out.

3 * Open the beer and pour out a couple of ounces. Place the chicken upright on the beer can. Put the beer can on the rack over the drip pan. Cover the grill and cook over indirect heat about 1 hour or until the juices run clear.

NOTE: This chicken can also be roasted in a 350°F oven. Just stand the beer can in a shallow roasting pan and roast about 1 hour or until the juices run clear.

BEER CAN TURKEY: Prepare recipe as directed, except substitute a 12-pound turkey for the chicken and use an extra-large beer can (such as Foster's) instead of a 12-ounce beer can. Grill turkey for 2½ hours or until the juices run clear. If the cover of your grill doesn't close completely when cooking a turkey, simply cover the open area with heavy-duty foil, creating a good seal around the grill.

BEER CAN GAME HEN: Prepare recipe as directed, except substitute a 1½- to 2-pound game hen. Stretch the cavity to make it larger and gently force the can into the cavity. Grill game hen for ½ hour or until the juices run clear.

game hen

chicken

turkey

SWEET-AND-SOUR PORK KEBABS

PREP: 20 minutes / GRILL: 15 minutes / YIELD: 4 servings

The marriage of apples and pork is a tender, succulent culinary classic—highly deserving of a good skewering!

1 tablespoon rice vinegar
1 tablespoon apricot preserves
1 teaspoon tomato paste
½ teaspoon chili powder
   Nonstick cooking spray
1 (1-pound) pork tenderloin
   Kosher salt or table salt and freshly
      ground black pepper, to taste
2 medium apples (Fuji or Granny
      Smith), cored
6 skewers
   Orange slices (optional)

1* For the glaze, mix together the vinegar, preserves, tomato paste, and chili powder; set aside. Coat the rack of a charcoal or gas grill with nonstick cooking spray. Preheat the grill to medium heat.

2* Cut the pork tenderloin into 1-inch cubes; season with salt and pepper. Cut the apples into the same size pieces. Alternate the pork and apple pieces on skewers.

3* Grill the kebabs directly over medium heat about 3 minutes on each side or until the pork is no longer pink. Brush the glaze generously on each kebab and cook for 30 seconds more on each side. Serve with orange slices, if desired.

Useless Fact: Pork tenderloin is as low in saturated fat as a chicken breast, but more tender and flavorful. Look for it in convenient packaged varieties in your supermarket and commence kebab-ing!

LOLLI-KEBABS

SOAK: 30 minutes / PREP: 10 minutes / GRILL: 5 minutes / YIELD: 16 kebabs

I grew up inhaling Armenian "loolleh-kebabs," but this bite-size version was just begging for a little creative re-spelling. These hors d'oeuvres are ideal for all your carnivorous guests—or any meat-on-a-stick fan in your life.

8	sets wooden chopsticks
2	pounds ground beef
1	large onion, finely chopped (1 cup)
¼	cup snipped fresh parsley
2	tablespoons tomato paste
1	teaspoon ground cumin
1	teaspoon paprika
	Kosher salt or table salt and freshly ground black pepper
	Nonstick cooking spray
	Pita bread
	Mint Sauce
	Cucumber slices (optional)

1* Soak 8 sets of wooden chopsticks in water for 30 minutes. Preheat a charcoal or gas grill to medium heat.

2* In a large bowl combine the beef, onion, parsley, tomato paste, cumin, and paprika; season generously with salt and pepper. Mix with your hands until well combined.

3* Form about ¼ cup of the meat mixture into a 2-inch-long hot dog shape on the narrow end of each chopstick. Coat with nonstick cooking spray. Grill directly over medium heat, turning frequently, about 5 minutes or until done (160°F). (Or cook the kebabs in a large nonstick skillet over medium-high heat about 5 minutes or until done [160°F].) Serve kebabs with pita bread, Mint Sauce, and, if desired, cucumber slices.

MINT SAUCE: In a small bowl mix 1 cup whole-milk plain yogurt; 1 tablespoon water; 5 mint leaves, finely chopped; and a pinch of kosher salt. Serve with the kebabs.

GEORGE'S SECRET ⌄

Make longer kebabs and serve them on hot dog buns with grilled onions and sweet peppers. It's an Armenian take on the classic Italian sausage sandwich!

GRILLED MEAT WITH GUASACACA SAUCE

PREP: 15 minutes / STAND: 1 hour / YIELD: 4 servings

Here's the plan: Get yourself invited to the next neighborhood barbecue. Make a batch of my guasacaca sauce and tell everyone to drizzle it over everything—meat, chicken, fish—even vegetables and potatoes! Bask in their immediate adulation as you become a neighborhood hero! (Then tell everyone to buy my book.)

1 medium onion, coarsely chopped (½ cup)
2 green sweet peppers, seeded and coarsely chopped (1½ cups)
2 ripe avocados, peeled and seeded
2 cloves garlic
½ bunch fresh parsley
½ bunch fresh cilantro
⅓ cup red wine vinegar
1 tablespoon kosher salt or 2 teaspoons table salt, or to taste
¼ teaspoon freshly ground black pepper
1 cup olive oil
 Desired grilled meat (such as skirt steak, ribs, and/or sausage)

1* For the guasacaca sauce, in a food processor combine the onion, sweet pepper, avocados, garlic, parsley, cilantro, vinegar, the 1 tablespoon salt, and the ¼ teaspoon black pepper; process until almost smooth. With the processor running, add the oil in a thin stream; process until smooth. Let stand at room temperature for at least 1 hour for the flavors to blend. Taste and adjust seasoning.

2* Meanwhile, prepare and grill desired meat.

3* Serve sauce with meat. Cover the leftover sauce and store in the refrigerator for up to 1 week. Bring sauce to room temperature before serving.

This sauce is pretty tasty but doesn't pack any heat, so if your tongue requires some spicy action, feel free to throw in a hot pepper or two.

CHEESESTEAK PIZZA

PREP: 15 minutes / COOK: 7 minutes / GRILL: 16 minutes / YIELD: 8 servings

When I first heard about grilling raw pizza dough, I was more than a little intimidated. But you have my word—not only is it easier than it looks—it's faster and tastier than making it in your oven! One of my favorite variations is the Cheesesteak Pizza. But remember, your pizza is your canvas!

1 tablespoon olive oil
1 medium onion, sliced
1 medium green sweet pepper, sliced
8 ounces cooked roast beef, thinly sliced
3 tablespoons Worcestershire sauce
¼ teaspoon freshly ground black pepper
1 pound prepared pizza dough (look for it in the frozen foods section of your supermarket)
 Olive oil
½ cup prepared tomato sauce
8 slices American cheese, chopped
8 ounces shredded mozzarella cheese (2 cups)

1* In a large skillet heat the 1 tablespoon oil over medium-high heat. Add the onion and sweet pepper; cook for 5 to 6 minutes or until the onion is soft and translucent. Add the roast beef; cook 2 to 3 minutes more. Use two forks to shred the beef. Stir in the Worcestershire sauce and black pepper; remove from heat.

2* Heat a charcoal or gas grill to medium-high heat. Divide pizza dough in half. Using your hands, pat and spread one-half of the pizza dough until it is ¼ inch thick. (It will make a 10- to 12-inch pizza.) Brush one side with olive oil. Place the crust, oil side down, on the grill rack. Brush with additional oil; cover grill. Grill about 5 minutes or until the bottom of the crust is browned and the top is set. Flip the crust over; cook on the other side about 3 minutes until browned. Remove crust from heat; set aside. Repeat with the remaining dough to make a second crust.

3* Spread each crust with half of the tomato sauce and half of the meat mixture. Top each with half of the American cheese and half of the mozzarella. Grill, covered, about 5 to 6 minutes or until the cheese is melted and bubbling.

MAKE-AHEAD TIP: Make your pizza crusts in advance, pile them up, and wrap them in foil. As your guests arrive, find out what topping they prefer and grill the crusts. They'll instantly crisp back up!

Grilling pizza is easier than you think. Just remember to oil the dough generously and make sure the grill is hot. Don't flip the crust until you can see browned grill marks on the dough.

CHIPOTLE CORN BITES

PREP: 10 minutes / GRILL: 10 minutes / YIELD: 4 to 6 servings

When I feel like sharing my love of this Mexican classic, I simply transform it into this easy, eat-with-your-fingers treat for my guests.

4   ears fresh corn with husks
1   cup low-fat mayonnaise
2   teaspoons adobo sauce,
         or to taste
1   tablespoon lime juice
1   tablespoon water
½   bunch fresh cilantro, finely snipped
       Kosher salt or table salt, to taste
½   cup shredded part-skim mozzarella
         cheese or queso fresco

1*Preheat a charcoal or gas grill to high heat. Grill the corn in the husks directly over the heat about 10 minutes or until charred all over, turning frequently. (Or roast the corn directly on the rack of a 400°F oven for 20 to 25 minutes.)

2*For the dipping sauce, whisk together the mayonnaise, adobo sauce, lime juice, water, cilantro, and salt. Remove the husks from the corn, reserving the husks for garnish (see below). Trim the ends off the corn and cut each ear into 1½-inch pieces. Pierce one of the cut ends of each piece with a toothpick or corn holder. Lightly spin each piece in the dipping sauce, sprinkle with cheese, and place on a platter.

Instead of throwing away the corn husks, fan them out on a platter and serve your corn bites on top.

edible
vegetable
skewers

PREP: 30 minutes
GRILL: 6 minutes
YIELD: 15 skewers

Coming from the kebab-loving Armenian culture, I have the utmost respect for the skewer. What better way to celebrate this remarkable culinary tool than by making it edible?

½ cup extra virgin olive oil
2 tablespoons garlic powder
3 tablespoons kosher salt or
   2 tablespoons table salt
1 tablespoon ground cumin
1 tablespoon ground coriander
1 tablespoon paprika
1 tablespoon freshly
   ground black pepper
1 teaspoon cayenne pepper
3 small zucchini
3 small yellow squash
15 baby carrots

1* In a medium bowl mix the olive oil, garlic powder, 1 tablespoon of the salt, the cumin, coriander, paprika, black pepper, and cayenne pepper until well blended; set aside.

2* Cut the zucchini and squash in half lengthwise; scrape out the seeds with a spoon. Place the vegetables, skin sides down, on a sheet pan. Sprinkle with the remaining 2 tablespoons salt; let stand for 5 minutes. Rinse in cold water and pat dry with paper towels. Slice crosswise into 1-inch pieces. Using the narrow end of a chopstick, gently form a hole through the center of each piece. Brush with the spice mixture and let stand while you prepare the carrots.

3* Using a peeler, trim the baby carrots to the width of a chopstick, leaving the top 1 inch of the carrot to use as a handle. Gently push a piece of zucchini onto the carrot with the skin side facing the top of the carrot. Skewer a piece of squash at a 90-degree angle to the zucchini. Repeat so there are two pieces each of zucchini and squash on the carrot skewer. Repeat until all the carrots have been used.

4* Preheat a charcoal or gas grill to medium-high heat. Place the skewers on the grill and cook directly over the heat for 3 minutes on each side or until the vegetables are tender.

GRILLED GARLIC AND BASIL POTATO PACKETS

PREP: 15 minutes / GRILL: 12 minutes / STAND: 5 minutes / YIELD: 4 packets

When you're grilling for a large crowd, making these potato packets saves you cooking time and dishwashing time. Make them right before grilling the meat, then just serve 'em up with a fork.

1 pound Red Bliss potatoes, washed
1 medium onion, finely chopped (½ cup)
5 large cloves garlic, forced through a garlic press or finely chopped
1 cup loosely packed fresh basil, coarsely chopped
3 tablespoons olive oil
  Kosher salt or table salt and freshly ground black pepper, to taste

1* Preheat a charcoal or gas grill to high heat. Tear off four 24×18-inch pieces of heavy-duty foil; fold in half to make four 12×18-inch rectangles.

2* Thinly slice the potatoes into a large bowl. Add the onion, garlic, basil, and oil; season with salt and pepper. Mix well. Divide the potato mixture evenly among the foil sheets, placing it in the centers. Bring up the long edges of the foil and seal with a double fold. Fold the remaining edges together to completely enclose the potatoes, leaving space for steam to build. Grill directly over the heat for 6 to 8 minutes on each side. Let stand for 5 minutes before serving.

MYSTERY THINGAMAJIGS ⌄

Can't stand the suspense of what's happening in that packet? The Qbag is your window into the world of foil cooking!

GRILLED GREEN BEAN CASSEROLE

PREP: 15 minutes / GRILL: 6 minutes / STAND: 5 minutes / YIELD: 6 servings

Just because it's grilling season doesn't mean you can't get your casserole on. Follow these instructions carefully and you'll be dishing up this American classic at your next barbecue. Seriously, you will!

6 cups fresh green beans,
    cut into 1-inch pieces
1 large portobello mushroom, chopped
1 cup condensed cream of
    mushroom soup
6 tablespoons butter, cut up
1 (1-ounce) package onion soup mix
3 cloves garlic, forced through
    a garlic press or finely chopped
    Kosher salt or table salt and freshly
    ground black pepper, to taste
1 (2.8-ounce) can french fried onions

1* Preheat a charcoal or gas grill to high heat. Cut six 18×18-inch pieces of foil. Fold in half to make rectangles; fold the rectangles in half to form squares. Close three sides of the squares with double folds to form packets.

2* In a large bowl mix the green beans with the mushroom, mushroom soup, butter, onion soup mix, and garlic. Season with salt and pepper. Spoon the mixture into the aluminum packets; seal.

3* Place the packets on the grill directly over the heat and cook for 3 to 4 minutes on each side. Let stand about 5 minutes. Open the packets and sprinkle with the onions.

Useless Fact: The green bean casserole was invented by the Campbell Soup Company to promote its cream of mushroom soup.

GRILLED BANANA SPLIT SUNDAES

SOAK: 30 minutes / PREP: 35 minutes / GRILL: 5 minutes / COOK: 5 minutes / YIELD: 8 to 10 servings

My devotion to banana splits knows no bounds. So why would I let the fact that I'm grilling prevent me from expressing my affection? This dessert is a delicious, creative wrap-up to a tasty, traditional cookout.

8   to 10 wooden skewers
2   to 3 bananas
1   frozen pound cake, thawed
1   whole pineapple
    About 20 maraschino cherries
¼   cup butter (½ stick), melted
2   cups whipping cream
9   ounces semisweet
       chocolate, chopped
    Vanilla ice cream

1 * Soak skewers in water for at least 30 minutes. Preheat a charcoal or gas grill to medium heat. Peel the bananas and cut into ½-inch slices. Trim the top off the pound cake and cut the rest into ½-inch cubes. Cut the top and bottom off the pineapple and remove the peel. Cut the pineapple into quarters. Trim the core and cut each piece again lengthwise. Cut the strips into ½-inch pieces.

2 * On a wooden skewer alternate pieces of banana, pound cake, pineapple, and cherries, leaving about 2 inches at one end. Brush with melted butter. Grill directly over medium heat for 1 to 2 minutes on each side. (Or broil the skewers about 1 to 2 minutes per side.)

3 * Meanwhile, for the sauce, heat the cream in a small pan over medium heat; do not boil. Add the chocolate to the warm cream. Let stand for a few minutes; stir to melt the chocolate. Cool a few minutes; pour into a squeeze bottle.

4 * Scoop ice cream into bowls and top with skewers. Squeeze chocolate sauce over the ice cream and fruit.

George's Secret: To bring extra zing to your sundae, top it with different colors and flavors of maraschino cherries!

cherry   passion fruit   lemon   lime   blueberry

CAMPFIRE ORANGE CINNAMON BUNS

PREP: 20 minutes / COOK: 7 minutes / YIELD: 5 servings

When I tell my fellow campers that I'm going to bake these babies in the fire, they look at me like I've lost my mind. But once I pull out the first batch of piping hot buns, they lose *their* minds from the delicious aroma and the stampede is on!

5 oranges
5 tablespoons packed brown sugar
1½ teaspoons ground cinnamon
1 (12-ounce) package refrigerated
    buttermilk biscuits (10)
10 tablespoons milk

1* Cut the top one-third off the oranges and scoop out all the pulp; reserve the tops for this recipe and, if desired, reserve the pulp for another use.

2* In a small bowl mix together the brown sugar and cinnamon. For each orange, flatten 2 rounds of biscuit dough; top with 1 tablespoon of the brown sugar mixture. Roll the biscuits into a ball and place in the oranges. (Note: The dough should fill the orange about two-thirds of the way, leaving room for the bun to expand. Add more or less dough according to the size of your orange.)

3* Add 2 tablespoons milk to each orange and cover with the orange tops. Wrap the oranges individually in three layers of foil. Put them into the glowing embers of the campfire to cook for 7 to 10 minutes, turning halfway through the cooking time. Wear gloves at all times to protect your hands from the fire.

SO THAT'S HOW YOU DO IT ⌄

It takes a strong spoon (and hand) to scrape out the oranges. Be careful not to rip through the peel.

GRILLED APPLE CRISP

PREP: 15 minutes / GRILL: 8 minutes / YIELD: 4 servings

There's nothing quite like the smell of apple crisp baking in the oven. But there's really nothing quite like the smell—and taste—of apple crisp cooked on the grill!

2   baking apples (Fuji or Gala),
     peeled and thinly sliced
1   cup dry bread crumbs
¼   cup packed dark brown sugar
1   teaspoon ground cinnamon
¼   cup butter (½ stick),
     cut into small pieces
     Vanilla ice cream (optional)

1 * Preheat a charcoal or gas grill to medium heat. Cut 4 large pieces of heavy-duty foil.

2 * In a large bowl toss the apples with the bread crumbs, brown sugar, and cinnamon. Place about ½ cup of the apple mixture on the center of each piece of foil. Top each with 1 tablespoon butter. Seal and gently flatten each packet. Grill directly over the heat for 8 to 10 minutes, turning once. (Or bake the packets in a 350°F oven for 20 to 25 minutes.) Cut packets open with scissors. Serve apple crisp directly in the foil packet or place packet contents in a bowl. If desired, serve with vanilla ice cream.

GEORGE'S SECRET ∨

If you serve this in the foil packets, use plastic spoons and forks. A metal spoon or fork can tear the foil, which could then end up lodged in a guest's throat. This is known in the party circuit as a "mood killer" or a "lawyer's feast."

THE PERFECT PARTY IS WITHIN YOUR GRASP. WITH RECIPES THAT REINVENT FAMILIAR FINGER FOODS AND HOIST THE HUMBLE LIBATION TO THE NEXT LEVEL IN LUSCIOUSNESS, YOUR BASH WILL PACK PLENTY OF CULINARY PUNCH.

THE BACON NUPTIALS OF '92

When I go to a wedding, the things I look forward to the most (besides doing the electric slide with the bride's great-aunt Fern) are the appetizers. The French term for appetizer is *amuse-bouche*, which—literally translated—means "mouth amuser." My love of all things mouth amusing was actually born from a circumstance where they were the main meal.

You see, all through high school I toiled as a part-time wedding videographer. This job not only prepared me for a career in showbiz but with a culinary education as well, courtesy of the seemingly endless parade of delectable taste treats available during the "hors d'oeuvres hour." Now even though I wasn't technically a guest at these weddings, as a fledgling artiste de video, I felt that the way to effectively communicate the assembled celebrants' experience was to immerse myself in that experience. Especially if they were experiencing something wrapped in BACON.

Which is why I will never forget the Hoover-Bryant nuptials of November 1992. It was as if we were soul mates. Fated to meet, destined to express our shared, eternal devotion to all things encased in this peerless pork product! Because amidst what was a dizzying array of appetizers (too many to count), **I was able to sink my teeth into not just the classic scallops but bacon-wrapped shrimp, beef tenderloin, asparagus, artichoke hearts, water chestnuts, and (perhaps my all-time favorites) dates! I was like a kid in a pork store!**

The rest of the evening was a blur. I floated through the reception on a smoke-cured cloud, my highly amused mouth frozen in an ear-to-ear grin as I happily captured video memories for the newlyweds. And while I can't conclusively prove that it was the power of bacon, it was, in my opinion, the finest reception footage I ever shot.

GRANNY SMITH GUACAMOLE

PREP: 10 minutes / YIELD: 8 to 10 servings

I could eat guacamole all day. In fact, on March 12, 2003, I did! That was the day I introduced the sweet tartness of diced Granny Smith apples to my famous guacamole. It was a revelation! Whip up a batch for your friends. They'll beg you for the recipe. But don't talk with your mouth full—just buy them a copy of my book!

3   ripe avocados, halved and pitted
½   cup finely chopped Vidalia onion
½   cup snipped fresh cilantro
     Juice of 1 lime
     Bottled hot pepper sauce, to taste
1   Granny Smith apple, peeled,
       cored, and finely chopped
     Kosher salt or table salt, to taste
     Assorted dippers (such as baked
       fruit crisps, apple chips,
       and/or tortilla chips)

1* Scoop avocado flesh into a bowl; add the onion, cilantro, lime juice, and hot pepper sauce. Mash with a fork until it reaches the desired consistency. Stir in apple and season with salt to taste. Serve with assorted dippers.

Useless Fact: There is an actual person named Granny Smith! Australian Maria Ann Smith unknowingly cultivated the first version of her namesake fruit from some crabapple seeds in her garden around 1865.

MEDITERRANEAN ARTICHOKE DIP

PREP: 15 minutes / BAKE: 6 minutes / YIELD: 10 to 12 servings

I understand the allure of sour cream-based dips. But believe me when I tell you that this Mediterranean dip uses the power of the artichoke to deliver a healthier and tastier alternative to the classic sour cream.

1 French bread baguette,
    cut into ½-inch slices
  Olive oil
1 (9-ounce) package frozen
    artichokes, thawed
½ cup coarsely snipped fresh parsley
¼ cup coarsely snipped fresh cilantro
½ cup pimiento-stuffed olives, chopped
1 clove garlic, forced through
    a garlic press or finely chopped
1 teaspoon bottled hot pepper sauce
  Kosher salt or table salt and freshly
    ground black pepper, to taste
  Assorted dippers (such as sweet
    pepper strips, tomato slices,
    and/or chips) (optional)

1* Preheat the oven to 350°F. Lightly brush both sides of the bread slices with oil; arrange on a baking sheet. Bake for 6 to 8 minutes or until lightly browned, turning once.

2* In a food processor combine the artichokes, parsley, and cilantro; process until finely chopped. Transfer the mixture to a bowl and stir in the olives, garlic, and hot pepper sauce. Season with salt and pepper. Serve with the toasted bread and, if desired, other assorted dippers.

SO THAT'S HOW YOU DO IT ⌄

Guests too lazy to actually dip? Try this instant appetizer! Just cut off the tops of cherry tomatoes and cut a sliver from the bottom of each (so they can stand upright). Gently scoop out the insides of the tomatoes with your finger. Then just fill each tomato with some of the dip.

candied camembert

PREP: 10 minutes / COOK: 15 minutes
YIELD: 8 to 10 servings

As the hot caramel cools, the ridiculously rich cheese inside the rind melts, leaving a gooey, cheesy treat for your guests to enjoy.

1 (8-ounce) wheel Camembert, at room temperature
½ cup sugar
2 tablespoons water
Crusty French bread or crackers

1* Remove the top rind of the Camembert. Using a knife, poke 8 to 10 holes in the top of the cheese. Put it on a glass serving plate.

2* Combine the sugar and water in a small heavy saucepan. Bring to a boil over medium heat and cook until thick and amber in color. (Use caution when working with hot sugar mixture and don't leave it untended.) Pour the hot mixture evenly over the Camembert. Serve immediately with bread or crackers.

PB&J JALAPEÑO POPPERS

PREP: 20 minutes / BAKE: 30 minutes / YIELD: 24 appetizers

I created these treats when *Ham on the Street* went to Vegas, where they brought a small measure of joy to disgruntled gamblers up and down the strip. They're great for anyone who suffers from jalapeño panic, because the nutty sweetness of the peanut butter and jelly really mellows out the pepper.

24   jalapeño chile peppers
     Disposable foil baking pan
1   cup chunky peanut butter
¼   cup jelly

1* Preheat the oven to 350°F. Wearing plastic gloves to protect your hands from pepper oils, cut the tops off the peppers and remove the membranes and seeds.

2* To make the pepper-holding pan, invert a disposable foil baking pan. To make each hole, pierce the foil pan with a sharp knife in an X. Press back foil pieces to create a square hole. Repeat to make 24 holes total. Place inverted foil pan on a baking sheet. Place a jalapeño pepper in each hole.

3* Put the peanut butter in a small zip-top plastic bag. Seal the bag and cut off a corner. Squeeze the peanut butter into the peppers, making sure that they are filled to the bottom. Top each with 1 teaspoon of your favorite jelly. Bake for 30 to 40 minutes or until the peppers are softened.

MYSTERY THINGAMAJIGS ∨

Seeding jalapeños can leave your hands feeling fried. Literally. That's why I consider this pepper corer a gift direct from the cooking gods.

CAESAR SALAD SUMMER ROLLS

PREP: 20 minutes / YIELD: 6 servings

To every kid who felt his mother's wrath every time he ate salad with his fingers: I feel your pain. Now our long struggle is over—Caesar salad has gone handheld.

1 head romaine lettuce
2 tablespoons anchovy paste
1 tablespoon Dijon-style mustard
2 cloves garlic, forced through a garlic press or finely chopped
Juice of 1 lemon
½ cup extra virgin olive oil
¼ cup freshly grated Parmesan cheese
12 (8-inch) Vietnamese rice paper sheets
¾ cup small croutons

1* Chop the lettuce into ½-inch pieces and put in a bowl. For the dressing, in a small bowl whisk together the anchovy paste, mustard, garlic, and lemon juice; whisk in the oil. Toss the lettuce with half of the dressing and all the Parmesan cheese.

2* Fill a large bowl with hot tap water. Dip a sheet of rice paper into the water for 10 to 15 seconds. (If the rice paper sheet is not pliable enough, it will break.) Once the rice paper is softened, place it on a large plate. Place 2 to 3 tablespoons of the salad just below the center of the sheet; add 4 or 5 croutons. Fold the bottom of the sheet over the salad, then fold the sides over the salad. Roll up from the bottom. Set aside, covered with a damp towel to keep the rolls from drying out while you make the rest. Serve with the remaining dressing as a dipping sauce.

What's the difference between spring rolls and summer rolls? While both use a rice paper wrapping, summer rolls are not fried and are served cold. Spring rolls are fried and served piping hot.

HAWAIIAN NACHOS

PREP: 15 minutes / COOK: 5 minutes / BAKE: 5 minutes / YIELD: 4 to 6 servings

For those short on time and cash, just sit back and transport yourself to that luau in your mind with my nacho-ization of the iconic Hawaiian pizza!

2   tablespoons olive oil
1½ cups diced cooked ham
½   cup chopped red onion
½   cup chopped green sweet pepper
1½ cups shredded Monterey Jack cheese (6 ounces)
1½ cups shredded cheddar cheese (6 ounces)
5   cups large tortilla chips
1   (14.5-ounce) can diced tomatoes, drained
1½ cups diced fresh pineapple, drained

1* Preheat the oven to 400°F. In a nonstick skillet heat 1 tablespoon oil over medium-high heat. Add ham; cook and stir for 2 to 3 minutes or until browned. Transfer to a plate. Heat the remaining 1 tablespoon oil in the skillet. Add the onion and pepper; cook for 2 to 3 minutes or until just softened. Remove from heat and stir in the ham. In a bowl mix together the cheeses.

2* Place half the tortilla chips in the bottom of a 9×9×2-inch baking pan or 1½-quart baking dish. Sprinkle with half the cheese, half the ham mixture, half the tomatoes, and half the pineapple. Repeat layers, starting with the remaining tortilla chips. Bake for 5 to 8 minutes or until the cheese is melted and bubbling. Serve at once.

GEORGE'S SECRET ⌄

For those who demand the classic American flavor of process cheese food with nachos, replace the cheese with 8 ounces of Velveeta.

DEEP-FRIED HAMMED MAC AND CHEESE

PREP: 20 minutes / CHILL: 1 hour / COOK: 20 minutes / YIELD: 8 to 10 servings

How do you improve on one of the all-time great guilty pleasures? Fire up the deep-fat fryer! You have not lived until you've tried this guiltiest of pleasures. Just don't make it a habit.

1   (7-ounce) ham steak
2   tablespoons butter
½   cup milk
1   cup cut-up process cheese
    (such as Velveeta)
1   cup dried elbow macaroni,
    cooked and drained
½   cup shredded cheddar cheese
    Vegetable oil
1   cup seasoned bread crumbs

1* Cut the ham into ¼-inch cubes. In a nonstick skillet heat 1 tablespoon of the butter over medium-high heat. Add the ham; cook for 4 to 5 minutes or until browned. Drain on paper towels.

2* In a medium pan over medium heat combine the milk, the remaining 1 tablespoon butter, and process cheese. Cook just until the cheese melts (don't let it boil). Add the macaroni, cheddar cheese, and ham; mix well. Pour into a bowl and refrigerate for at least 1 hour or until firm.

3* In a deep-fat fryer heat oil to 375°F. (Or heat 2 inches of oil in a deep cast-iron skillet.)

4* Scoop the firm macaroni and cheese to form 2-inch balls. Roll in the bread crumbs. Fry the balls, a few at a time, for about 2 minutes or until golden brown. Drain on paper towels and serve immediately.

HOLY GRAIL OF OPTIONS ⌄

BOXED

DELI

FROZEN

Running low on time? Try starting with one of these instant mac and cheese alternatives. Just stir ⅓ cup melted Velveeta into 1 cup cooked instant product.

FRIED **BRIE BITES** WITH HONEY MUSTARD

PREP: 15 minutes / *COOK:* 5 minutes / *YIELD:* 4 servings

Once my deep-fat fryer gets going, there's no telling what I'll drop in there. Okay, okay, I'll tell you: Bits of rich, creamy Brie in a crispy bread crumb crust. Enjoy!

2 tablespoons whole-grain mustard
2 tablespoons honey
2 teaspoons red wine vinegar
Vegetable oil
½ cup all-purpose flour
1 cup panko (Japanese-style bread crumbs)
1 egg
1 (10-ounce) piece Brie, cut into bite-size pieces

1 * For the sauce, whisk together the mustard, honey, and vinegar; set aside. In a deep-fat fryer heat the oil to 350°F. (Or heat 2 inches of oil in a deep cast-iron skillet.)

2 * While the oil is heating, put the flour and panko on separate plates. In a small bowl beat the egg. Flour each bite of Brie, then dip into the egg. Press into the panko, making sure each bite is completely coated. (The coated Brie bites can be covered and refrigerated for up to 2 hours.)

3 * Fry the Brie bites, a few at a time, about 5 to 10 seconds or until browned. Drain on paper towels while you fry the rest. Serve immediately with the sauce.

GEORGE'S SECRET ∨

My rule is that if you can fry one thing, you can fry every last one of its close relations. Try the same recipe with cheddar, Camembert, Swiss, or any other semi-firm cheese.

SHOVEL OF CHÈVRE

PREP: 15 minutes / YIELD: about 20 appetizers

Go to any 99-cent store and you'll find inexpensive tablespoons that are easy to bend—spoons that make the ideal vehicle to serve delicate hors d'oeuvres like this at your next party.

2   ripe tomatoes, seeded and chopped
3   tablespoons extra virgin olive oil
2   teaspoons balsamic vinegar
2   teaspoons soy sauce
     Kosher salt or table salt and freshly
        ground black pepper, to taste
2   ounces fresh goat cheese, crumbled

1* In a bowl combine the chopped tomatoes, oil, vinegar, and soy sauce; season with salt and pepper.

2* Bend each spoon so the handle supports the edge of the spoon on a flat surface (see below). Add a teaspoon of the tomato mixture to each spoon and top with a few crumbles of goat cheese.

SO THAT'S HOW YOU DO IT ⌄

Tell Uri Geller his spoon-bending services won't be needed. Just follow these directions.

Bend #1 ↘

Bend #2 ↗

HERBED POLENTA FRIES

PREP: 25 minutes / CHILL: 2 hours / COOK: 15 minutes / YIELD: 4 to 6 servings

Like me, you've probably run the scenario "What will I do when aliens attack?" through your mind hundreds of times. Luckily I've got a lifesaver: Offer up a platter of these crunchy on the outside, creamy on the inside "fries." Instead of performing medical experiments on you, the aliens might hire you to cook for them!

Nonstick cooking spray
3   cups chicken stock or broth
2   tablespoons prepared pesto
1   cup quick polenta
1   cup shredded cheddar cheese
½   cup low-fat mayonnaise
2   teaspoons fresh lemon juice
1   clove garlic, forced through a
        garlic press or finely chopped
Kosher salt or table salt and freshly
        ground black pepper, to taste
Vegetable oil
3   tablespoons quick polenta
Snipped fresh herbs (such as oregano
        and/or Italian parsley) (optional)

1 * Coat a 9×5×3-inch loaf pan generously with nonstick cooking spray. In a medium pan bring the chicken stock to a simmer over medium-high heat. Stir in the pesto. Slowly pour in the 1 cup polenta, stirring constantly. Stir in the cheese. Turn the heat to low and continue cooking and stirring until the polenta is very thick. Quickly pour the polenta into the prepared pan and cover with plastic wrap, pressing the plastic wrap directly onto the surface of the polenta. Refrigerate for at least 2 hours or overnight until firm.

2 * For the lemon-garlic dipping sauce, stir together the mayonnaise, lemon juice, garlic, salt, and pepper, adding water 1 teaspoon at a time, if needed, until it is the consistency of whipping cream.

3 * Turn out the firm polenta onto a cutting board; cut into 5×½×½-inch strips. Heat ¼ inch oil in a skillet over medium-high heat. When it is hot (dip the end of a wooden spoon into the oil: if bubbles form, the oil is hot enough), coat the fries with the 3 tablespoons polenta. Carefully put the strips into the oil; fry about 5 minutes per side or until golden brown. Drain on paper towels. If desired, sprinkle with fresh snipped herbs. Serve with the lemon-garlic dipping sauce.

GEORGE'S SECRET ⌄

What's the difference between polenta and grits? Not a whole lot! Both are made from ground corn, though grits usually use hominy (a white corn with the hull and germ removed) rather than polenta's yellow corn (with the germ still there). The germ gives polenta a "cornier" flavor and limits its shelf life.

PASTA WITH MEATBALLS ON A STICK

PREP: 30 minutes / COOK: 10 minutes / BROIL: 10 minutes / YIELD: 80 meatballs

Hey, Pasta! You too, Meatballs. Are you tired of the same old bowl?
Then welcome to the wonderful world of food on a stick! You can
skip the marinara sauce recipe by using the store-bought kind.

1   (35-ounce) can crushed tomatoes
3   sprigs fresh thyme
1   bay leaf
1   tablespoon dried oregano, crushed
2   teaspoons garlic powder
⅛   teaspoon sugar
    Kosher salt or table salt and freshly
        ground black pepper, to taste
1   pound ground beef
1   pound ground pork
½   bunch fresh parsley, snipped
1   cup dry bread crumbs
1   tablespoon ground cumin
1   tablespoon dried oregano, crushed
2   eggs
6   ounces dried farfalle, large
        rotini, and/or mafalda pasta
2   tablespoons extra virgin olive oil
1   unripened melon
80 wooden skewers

1* For the marinara sauce, in a saucepan over medium heat combine the tomatoes, thyme, bay leaf, oregano, garlic powder, sugar, salt, and pepper. Simmer for 10 to 15 minutes.

2* Preheat the broiler. In a large bowl mix the beef and pork; add the parsley, bread crumbs, cumin, oregano, and eggs; season with salt and pepper. Mix well to combine. Roll 1 tablespoon of the mixture into a small ball; repeat to make about 80 small meatballs. Put them on a baking sheet; broil about 10 to 15 minutes or until they are browned and cooked through.

3* Cook the farfalle according to package directions. Drain and rinse in cold water. Toss with the oil.

4* On each skewer thread a farfalle and a meatball. To serve, cut an unripened melon in half lengthwise and put it cut side down on a platter. Insert the skewers into the melon. Serve with warm marinara sauce for dipping.

NOTE: For meatball faces, put ketchup in a small zip-top bag. Cut off one small corner of the bag. Pipe desired facial expressions on the meatballs.

DANTE'S DEVILED EGGS

PREP: 35 minutes / YIELD: 6 to 8 servings

Finally, some deviled eggs that bring enough spice to earn their diabolical designation. Hot-food lovers, prepare for an all-out egg-ferno that will transport your taste buds where you know they want to go—straight to HELL!

1   dozen eggs
5   tablespoons low-fat mayonnaise
2   tablespoons tomato paste with
        Italian herbs
2   to 3 teaspoons bottled hot pepper
        sauce
     Kosher salt or table salt and freshly
        ground black pepper, to taste
     Paprika (optional)

1 * Put the eggs in a large pan and cover by at least 2 inches with cold water. Put the pan over high heat. When it comes to a boil, remove from heat, cover, and let stand for about 15 minutes. Drain and run cold water over the eggs to stop the cooking. When cooled, remove the shells.

2 * Cut the eggs in half;* put the yolks into a bowl. Mash the yolks with the mayonnaise, tomato paste, and hot pepper sauce until smooth. Season to taste with salt and pepper. Place the yolk mixture in a zip-top plastic bag.** Just before serving, snip off one corner of the bag. Gently squeeze the bag and fill each egg white. Cover and chill until serving time. If desired, sprinkle with paprika.

*TIP: To keep your eggs from wobbling all over the serving tray, cut a sliver from the bottom of each egg half.

**NOTE: To kick up the presentation factor on these eggs, try piping the yolk mixture from a pastry bag fitted with a large star tip.

STUFFED **FIGS** IN A BLANKET

PREP: 25 minutes / BAKE: 20 minutes / YIELD: 12 pieces

When Peter, the writer for *Ham on the Street,* wondered if you could give dried fruit the turducken treatment, I wrote it off as one of his insane ramblings. Then, one night when I couldn't sleep, I actually concocted one. Turns out he's not insane— he's a mad genius!

¼ cup dried cranberries, chopped
6 ounces fresh goat cheese
   (at room temperature)
12 dried whole apricots
12 raisins
12 dried figs
6 slices prosciutto

1* Preheat the oven to 350°F. In a bowl combine the cranberries and the goat cheese. Cut the tops off the apricots and use your finger to create a pocket in each. Fill an apricot with some of the cheese mixture, then push a raisin into it.

2* Cut the tops off the figs and use your finger to create a pocket in each. Fill a fig with some of the cheese mixture, then push the stuffed apricot into it. Repeat until all the fruit has been used. Halve the prosciutto slices lengthwise; wrap a slice around each fig. Secure with a toothpick, if necessary. Place on a baking sheet; bake for 20 to 25 minutes or until the prosciutto has browned. Let cool slightly before serving.

To fully appreciate the creation you've concocted, take a look at this cross section.

prosciutto

apricot

raisin

goat cheese

fig   cranberry

APPLE-STRAWBERRY SANGRIA

PREP: 5 minutes / YIELD: about 10 servings

This white-wine sangria is a refreshing alternative to the ubiquitous red-wine version. Make sure to chop the apples and strawberries finely and serve each glass with a spoon, allowing your guests to sip and eat their way to happiness.

3   Granny Smith apples, cored
      and chopped
1   pint strawberries, hulled and chopped
5   cups orange-tangerine juice
      Juice of 2 oranges
1   bottle dry white wine
      (such as Pinot Grigio)
1   cup brandy
      Ice

1* In a large pitcher combine the apples, strawberries, juices, wine, and brandy; gently stir to mix. Add some ice. Pour into glasses, making sure to get some fruit in each one. Serve with spoons.

TIP: This drink is best served from a wide-mouth pitcher into small tumblers. Provide spoons so your guests can eat the fruit.

MANGO CHAMPAGNE COCKTAIL

PREP: 5 minutes / COOK: 2 minutes / STEEP: 1 hour / YIELD: 8 servings

I have always loved a classic Mexican street snack, mango on a stick. Here, the succulent sweetness of the mango plays perfectly off of the chili-powder coating—a flavor sensation that mixes amazingly well with Champagne. These killer cocktails will add serious spice to your next summer bash.

1 (12-ounce) can mango nectar
12 black peppercorns
1 cinnamon stick
2 star anise
2 whole cloves
½ teaspoon crushed red pepper
1 (750-milliliter) bottle Champagne
 or sparkling wine
 Mango slices (optional)

1* In a small saucepan bring the nectar to a boil over high heat. Reduce the heat to medium; cook for 2 minutes. Remove from the heat; add the peppercorns, cinnamon stick, star anise, cloves, and crushed red pepper. Let the mixture cool, then strain and refrigerate.

2* Spoon 2 tablespoons of the mango mixture into each champagne flute; top with chilled Champagne. If desired, garnish with mango slices.

Cava (a sparkling wine from Spain) is a cheaper alternative to Champagne and works perfectly with this drink.

MOJITO **GRANITA**

PREP: 15 minutes / COOK: 5 minutes / FREEZE: 4 hours / YIELD: 8 servings

For me, this is the best way to consume alcohol. Just make sure the glasses are frozen before serving because as delicious as granita is, it melts quickly.

1 cup sugar
3 cups water
1 bunch mint leaves (reserve some sprigs for garnish)
½ cup fresh lime juice
½ cup white rum

1* In a saucepan bring the sugar and water to a boil over medium-high heat. When the sugar has dissolved, remove from heat; let cool.

2* In a blender combine the mint leaves, lime juice, rum, and the cooled sugar syrup. Blend for 30 to 45 seconds or until the mint is finely chopped. Pour mixture into a 13x9x2-inch baking pan; place in freezer. Scrape the mixture every hour with a fork to break up the ice crystals. After about 4 to 6 hours the pan will be full of mojito ice flakes and will be ready to serve. Serve in small, chilled bowls or glasses. Garnish with reserved mint sprigs.

So many mints! There are about 500 varieties of mint in the world, including peppermint, spearmint, apple mint, orange mint, Spanish mint, pineapple mint, ginger mint, lamb mint, lemon mint, pennyroyal, water mint, chocolate mint. . . .and the list goes on.

GREEN TEA MARTINI

PREP: 5 minutes / *STEEP:* 5 minutes / *COOL:* 30 minutes / *YIELD:* 2 servings

Tired of falling asleep on your third martini? With a dash of that elixir of life known as green tea, your buddy George saves the day. Cheers!

½   cup hot water
2   green tea bags or
     2 tablespoons loose green tea
     Ice
½   cup vodka
2   ounces orange liqueur
     (such as Cointreau)
2   tablespoons honey
     Mint sprigs (optional)
     Citrus curls (optional)

1* Pour the hot water over the green tea, cover, and let steep for 5 minutes. Remove the bags (or strain out the leaves); let tea stand about 30 minutes or until cool.

2* Fill a cocktail shaker with ice. Add the tea, vodka, orange liqueur, and honey. Shake well; serve in chilled martini glasses. Garnish with mint and citrus curls, if desired.

CINNAMON-BANANA MILK SHAKE

PREP: 5 minutes / YIELD: 2 servings

When you grow up in South America, the fresh fruit shakes known as *batidas* are a mouthwatering way of life. There were almost limitless combinations, but this one was perhaps my all-time favorite.

2 scoops vanilla ice cream
1 cup milk
2 ripe bananas
1 teaspoon ground cinnamon
1 vanilla bean or ½ teaspoon
vanilla extract
Fresh fruit skewer (optional)

1* In a blender combine the ice cream, milk, bananas, and cinnamon. Scrape the seeds from the vanilla bean with the back of a knife and add to the ice cream mixture. Blend on high speed until smooth and frothy. If desired, garnish with skewers of fresh fruit.

HOLY GRAIL OF OPTIONS ⌄

PAPAYA

CANTALOUPE

Try replacing bananas with any one of these fruits for a frosty Caribbean delight!

PINEAPPLE

HONEY-ROSEMARY ICED TEA

PREP: 5 minutes / STEEP: 20 minutes / CHILL: 30 minutes / YIELD: 4 servings

This summer specialty can work with many different types of tea. The smokiness of the tea, the sweetness of the honey, and the tartness of the lemon give a three-pronged flavor sensation.

6 cups boiling water
14 sprigs fresh rosemary
6 Earl Grey tea bags
1 cup sugar
½ cup honey
1 cup fresh lemon juice
 Ice
 Fresh rosemary sprigs (optional)
 Lemon slices (optional)

1 * In a heatproof pitcher or bowl pour the boiling water over 10 of the rosemary sprigs. Let steep for 15 minutes. Add the tea bags; let steep for 5 minutes more. Remove and discard the rosemary and tea bags. Add the sugar, honey, and lemon juice; stir until dissolved. Chill for 30 minutes or until ready to serve. Serve in tall glasses filled with ice. If desired, garnish each with an additional sprig of rosemary and lemon slices.

Useless Fact: About 85% of all tea consumed in the United States is iced tea.

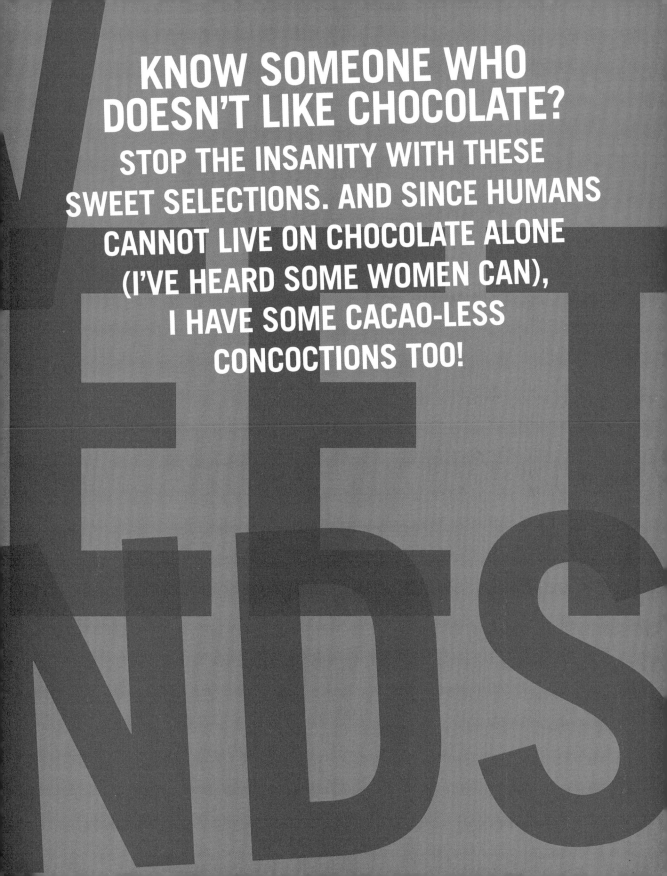

KNOW SOMEONE WHO DOESN'T LIKE CHOCOLATE? STOP THE INSANITY WITH THESE SWEET SELECTIONS. AND SINCE HUMANS CANNOT LIVE ON CHOCOLATE ALONE (I'VE HEARD SOME WOMEN CAN), I HAVE SOME CACAO-LESS CONCOCTIONS TOO!

WHAT MARSHMALLOWS?!?

People always remember their first kiss, their first love, their first broken heart. These are indelible memories that help shape who we are and how we see the world. But for some of us, there are other, similarly unforgettable firsts. Moments that, while not necessarily as poignant, exert an equally powerful influence upon this journey we call "life." For me, one of those moments is unquestionably my first sugar high.

I remember it like it was yesterday. No, make that ten minutes ago. I was but a lad, a mere 6 years of age, alone in the family kitchen. I had recently discovered the joys of everyone's favorite sweet, cushiony treat—the marshmallow. And even more recently (maybe five minutes before), I'd discovered where my mom hid them. When a fortuitous phone call took her away to the living room, one thing was clear: I needed to make my move.

I worked with precision, focus, and efficiency—letting each marshmallow meander briefly around my mouth, softening just enough to release its decadent essence—before I slurped it down. One by one, they disappeared, until suddenly all I had left was an empty plastic bag and a feeling of utter invincibility!

I hadn't intended to finish the bag. But once I got started, I can only remember one thing: never wanting this wonderful feeling to end. I didn't count how many marshmallows perished that day but judging from my mother's reaction when she found the empty bag, it was a lot. But I didn't care how mad my mom was—I had opened a door to dessert debauchery that would be impossible to close.

While many might disagree, I consider that simple act of childhood gluttony my first recipe: "Marshmallow Surprise." And though I would never "prepare" it again, the feeling it gave me provides inspiration to this day. Inspiration to craft creative desserts that can put a sinfully sweet exclamation point at the end of your meal.

DEEP-FRIED CHOCOLATE CHIP COOKIE DOUGH

PREP: 25 minutes / FREEZE: 30 minutes / COOK: 15 minutes / YIELD: about 36 balls

Growing up (and hell, even today!), the only thing better than my mom's chocolate chip cookies was the dough. Now there's something better than that—thanks to my good friend, the deep-fryer. Get ready for the gooey fun!

2½   cups all-purpose flour
1   teaspoon baking soda
1   teaspoon salt
1   cup butter (2 sticks), softened
1½   cups packed brown sugar
½   cup granulated sugar
½   cup pasteurized egg (Egg Beaters)
1   teaspoon vanilla
1   12-ounce package (2 cups)
     chocolate chips
2   cups all-purpose flour
2   tablespoons granulated sugar
1   teaspoon baking powder
¼   cup pasteurized egg
¾   cup seltzer water or club
     soda, plus more if needed
     Vegetable oil
     Powdered sugar

1 * For the dough: In a bowl stir together the 2½ cups flour, the baking soda, and salt; set aside. In a mixing bowl beat the butter with an electric or hand mixer until it is lighter in color. Add the brown sugar and the ½ cup granulated sugar; beat until light and fluffy. Add the egg half at a time and beat until incorporated. Stir in the vanilla. Beat in the flour mixture, then stir in the chocolate chips.

2 * For each cookie, roll 2 teaspoons of the dough into a ball. Put the balls on a cookie sheet. Freeze for 30 minutes or until firm.

3 * For the batter, in a large bowl whisk together the 2 cups flour, 2 tablespoons granulated sugar, and baking powder. Add the egg and half the seltzer; whisk to combine. Add more seltzer as needed until the batter is the consistency of heavy cream.

4 * In a deep-fat fryer heat the oil to 375°F. Dip the chilled dough balls in the batter, then carefully place them in the hot oil. Fry, a few at a time, for 2 to 3 minutes or until golden brown, turning them over from time to time. Drain on paper towels. Sprinkle with powdered sugar and serve warm.

SO THAT'S HOW YOU DO IT ⌄

Pamper your guests by using a fine sieve and powdered sugar to add a decadent layer of dust to these delectable goodies.

HOT AND SPICY BROWNIES

PREP: 15 minutes / BAKE: 15 minutes / YIELD: 24 mini brownies

The smoky spice of chipotle peppers adds a surprising and delicious twist to this timeless chocolate treat. Just make sure to serve it with plenty of milk!

½ cup (1 stick) butter
3 (1-ounce) squares unsweetened chocolate
1 cup sugar
2 eggs
2 canned chipotle peppers in adobo, chopped
1 teaspoon vanilla
¼ teaspoon salt
½ cup all-purpose flour
2 teaspoons five-spice powder

1 * Preheat the oven to 325°F. Lightly grease 24 mini muffin cups.

2 * In a double boiler or in a bowl set over a pan of simmering water melt the butter and the chocolate. Remove from heat and whisk in the sugar, eggs, chopped peppers, vanilla, and salt. Stir in the flour and five-spice powder until incorporated. Pour into mini muffin cups and bake about 15 minutes. (Or pour the batter into a greased 8×8×2-inch pan and bake about 30 minutes.)

NOTE: If you like it extra hot, try dusting these little bites with cayenne pepper. Eat at your own risk!

Useless Fact: Chipotle peppers in adobo (see above) are actually just jalapeño peppers that have been smoke-dried, then stewed in adobo sauce (made from tomatoes, garlic, vinegar, salt, and assorted spices). Cans of this flavorful item are now widely available in the Mexican section of most supermarkets.

LEMON-THYME OLIVE OIL COOKIES

PREP: 20 minutes / BAKE: 12 minutes / YIELD: 40 cookies

One of my favorite things to do is watch a doubter's eyes widen as he or she chews their first bite of these savory yet sweet, melt-in-your-mouth cookies. Just one more example of the power of olive oil!

2 cups all-purpose flour
1 cup sugar
1 tablespoon snipped
   fresh thyme
1 teaspoon freshly ground black pepper
½ teaspoon baking soda
½ cup extra virgin olive oil
3 tablespoons milk
   Zest and juice from 1 large lemon
   Powdered sugar (optional)

1 * Preheat the oven to 350°F. Line two baking sheets with parchment paper or silicone baking sheets.

2 * In a bowl stir together the flour, sugar, thyme, pepper, and baking soda. In a small bowl whisk together the olive oil, milk, lemon zest, and juice. Add the oil mixture to the flour mixture, stirring with a wooden spoon until a smooth dough forms.

3 * Roll heaping teaspoonfuls of the dough into balls. Place the balls about 2 inches apart on the prepared baking sheets. Bake for 12 to 15 minutes or until they are browned around the edges. Let the cookies cool on the baking sheet for a few minutes. Transfer to wire racks and cool completely. If desired, sprinkle with powdered sugar.

MYSTERY THINGAMAJIGS ⌄

If you ever make cookie cutouts, you can roll the dough and keep track of your cookie cutters with this rolling pin/cookie cutter storage bin!

RASPBERRY CHEESECAKE

BROWNIES

PREP: 10 minutes / BAKE: 32 minutes / YIELD: 16 to 20 brownies

Cheesecake or brownie? This dessert offers the perfect solution to those of you (like me) who refuse to decide between these two classics. It's definitely rich and decadent, but the raspberries bring a splash of fresh, fruity balance.

2 cups frozen raspberries, thawed
1 (8-ounce) package cream cheese, at room temperature
½ cup sugar
1 egg
2 tablespoons all-purpose flour
1 (19.5- to 21.2-ounce) package brownie mix
⅔ cup vegetable oil
2 eggs
2 tablespoons water

1* Preheat the oven to 350°F. Grease a 13x9x2-inch baking pan.

2* In a blender puree the raspberries until they are almost smooth. Strain, using a plastic spatula to press the berries through the sieve. (You should have 4 to 5 tablespoons of raspberry puree.)

3* In a medium mixing bowl beat the raspberry sauce, cream cheese, sugar, 1 egg, and flour with an electric mixer until smooth.

4* In a large bowl combine the brownie mix, oil, and 2 eggs. Pour two-thirds of the brownie mixture evenly into the prepared pan. Bake for 20 minutes. Remove pan from oven. Immediately top brownies with the raspberry mixture and spread gently. Add 2 tablespoons water to the remaining brownie mixture. Drizzle brownie mixture over raspberry mixture. Use a chopstick or a knife to make swirls throughout the batter.

5* Bake for 12 minutes longer or until a toothpick inserted in the center comes out clean. Cool in pan.

MYSTERY THINGAMAJIGS ⌄

There are two kinds of people in the world: those who live for the chewy, crusty goodness of "corner brownies" and those who weren't quick enough to grab 'em first. Now, thanks to the ingenious "brownie corner pan," getting the dreaded "middle piece" is not a problem!

ICE CREAM CLUB SANDWICH

PREP: 20 minutes / COOK: 10 minutes / YIELD: 4 sandwiches

The classic ice cream sandwich has a permanent place in the frozen dessert pantheon. But that doesn't mean I can't offer an alternative! With waffles for "bread" and raspberry coulis for "ketchup," this triple-decker club will take your taste buds to new heights!

8   frozen square waffles
1   cup fresh raspberries
1   half-gallon brick-style carton
     desired flavor ice cream
4   thin, crispy wafer cookies
     Mini chocolate chips and/or sprinkles
     Fresh raspberries
     Raspberry Coulis

1* Toast the frozen waffles according to package directions and let cool. Slice the raspberries in half.

2* Remove ice cream from carton. Cut eight ½-inch-thick square slices from the ice cream block. If desired, trim each square to fit waffle dimensions. Return all but two ice cream squares to freezer. Place the remaining two squares on each of two waffles. Cover one ice cream square with raspberry halves. Press a wafer cookie onto the other ice cream square. Gently press the two waffles together. Place in freezer while you make the remaining sandwiches.

3* Spread the chocolate chips on a plate. Remove the sandwiches from the freezer. Press edges of each sandwich into the chocolate chips. Carefully cut sandwiches in half using a serrated knife. Arrange on plates. Garnish with raspberries and serve with Raspberry Coulis.

RASPBERRY COULIS: In a small saucepan combine 1 (10-ounce) bag frozen unsweetened raspberries, ½ cup sugar, and 1 teaspoon fresh lemon juice. Cook over medium heat, stirring often to mash the berries, until their juices are released. Press through a sieve to strain out the seeds. Cover and store in the refrigerator for up to 3 days.

Also try using a ketchup squeeze bottle to garnish your sandwich with the coulis so that it looks like. . .ketchup!

CHOCOLATE-STRAWBERRY QUESADILLAS

PREP: 5 minutes / COOK: 4 minutes / YIELD: 2 servings

Like most people, I estimate that I spend one-third of my waking hours figuring out ways to incorporate chocolate into my meal. Oh, you don't do that too? That's okay, I'll do it for you! Feel free to use apples, blackberries, and mangoes here!

2   tablespoons chocolate-hazelnut spread (such as Nutella)
2   flour tortillas
3   large strawberries, hulled and sliced
Sliced strawberries (optional)

1 * Heat a nonstick skillet over medium heat. Spread the chocolate evenly on one tortilla and place it, chocolate side up, in the skillet. Arrange the strawberry slices over the chocolate and cover with the second tortilla. Cook about 2 minutes, then flip and cook about 2 minutes more. Slice into triangles. If desired, top with sliced strawberries.

SO THAT'S HOW YOU DO IT ⌄

Hulling strawberries is easy. Simply use the sharp end of a paring knife to cut a cone around the stem of the strawberry. Pull out the stem with the white and voilà!

MACADAMIA NUT BRITTLE

PREP: 5 minutes / COOK: 15 minutes / COOL: 30 minutes / YIELD: about 1 pound

If it's a nut, you can make it into a brittle. But why not start at the top, with the king of all nuts, the mighty macadamia—a rich, delicate, and oh-so-creamy complement to its sweet, crunchy surroundings.

1 cup sugar
1 cup light-colored corn syrup
1½ cups lightly toasted and crushed macadamia nuts

1 * Line a baking pan with a silicone baking sheet or buttered parchment paper. Set aside.

2 * In a heavy pan combine the sugar and corn syrup. Cook over medium heat until the sugar is dissolved, stirring often. Turn the heat to high and cook about 10 minutes or until the mixture turns a light amber color. Stir in the nuts and cook for 1 minute more.

3 * Quickly pour the mixture onto the prepared baking pan, spreading evenly with a spatula or wooden spoon. The mixture cools quickly so work fast. Let cool and break into pieces.

Useless Fact: Why are macadamia nuts so expensive? Because it's extremely hard to open the shell (the hardest one in all nut-dom) without smashing the nut to smithereens!

NACHO MAMA'S S'MORES

PREP: 5 minutes / BAKE: 5 minutes / YIELD: 6 to 8 servings

I love s'mores. But all too often I end up squeezing the graham cracker too hard and lose precious marshmallow and chocolate to the ground below. With this sinfully sweet plate of "nachos," you get far fewer drips and plenty of finger licks. Problem solved!

1 (14-ounce) package graham crackers
3 (5-ounce) milk chocolate bars
   (recommended: Hershey's)
½ of a (10.5-ounce) bag mini
   marshmallows

1 *Preheat the oven to 350°F. Break the graham crackers into pieces and place one-third of them in a layer in an ovenproof skillet or pie plate. Break up the chocolate bars and arrange one-third of them on top of the crackers. Add one-third of the marshmallows. Repeat layers twice. Bake for 5 to 8 minutes or until the marshmallows are light golden and the chocolate is melted.

Wanna freak out your friends? Well, I usually do. So I replace the marshmallows in this recipe with Peeps—those adorable little marshmallow chicks. Once they melt, let the visual fun begin!

forgotten chocolate soufflé

PREP: 30 minutes
BAKE: 30 minutes
YIELD: 8 to 10 servings

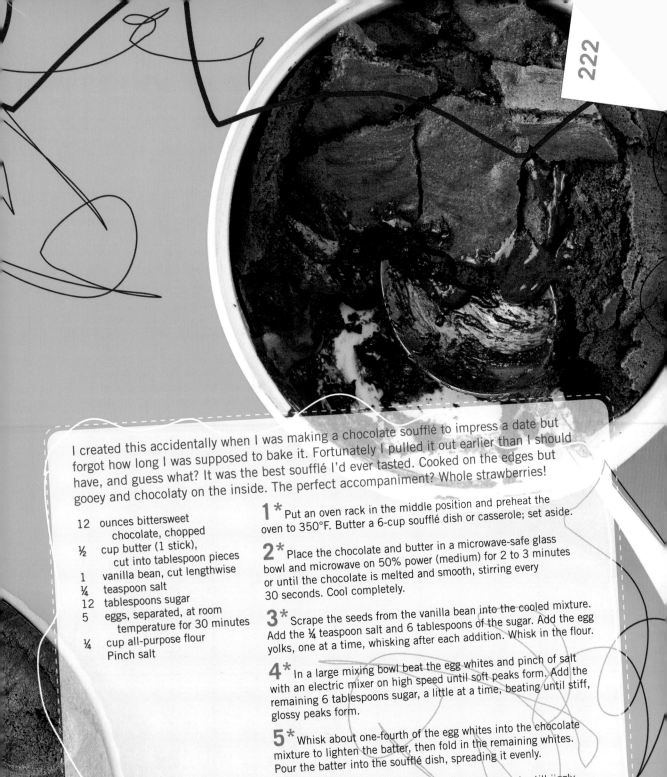

I created this accidentally when I was making a chocolate soufflé to impress a date but forgot how long I was supposed to bake it. Fortunately I pulled it out earlier than I should have, and guess what? It was the best soufflé I'd ever tasted. Cooked on the edges but gooey and chocolaty on the inside. The perfect accompaniment? Whole strawberries!

12	ounces bittersweet chocolate, chopped
½	cup butter (1 stick), cut into tablespoon pieces
1	vanilla bean, cut lengthwise
¼	teaspoon salt
12	tablespoons sugar
5	eggs, separated, at room temperature for 30 minutes
¼	cup all-purpose flour
	Pinch salt

1* Put an oven rack in the middle position and preheat the oven to 350°F. Butter a 6-cup soufflé dish or casserole; set aside.

2* Place the chocolate and butter in a microwave-safe glass bowl and microwave on 50% power (medium) for 2 to 3 minutes or until the chocolate is melted and smooth, stirring every 30 seconds. Cool completely.

3* Scrape the seeds from the vanilla bean into the cooled mixture. Add the ¼ teaspoon salt and 6 tablespoons of the sugar. Add the egg yolks, one at a time, whisking after each addition. Whisk in the flour.

4* In a large mixing bowl beat the egg whites and pinch of salt with an electric mixer on high speed until soft peaks form. Add the remaining 6 tablespoons sugar, a little at a time, beating until stiff, glossy peaks form.

5* Whisk about one-fourth of the egg whites into the chocolate mixture to lighten the batter, then fold in the remaining whites. Pour the batter into the soufflé dish, spreading it evenly.

6* Bake for 30 to 35 minutes or until the center is still jiggly and a toothpick inserted in the center comes out with moist crumbs. Serve warm.

MY MOM'S CHOCOLATE CHIP
COOKIE CAKE

PREP: 20 minutes / BAKE: 50 minutes / YIELD: 12 servings

Ever since I was a kid, my brother, sister, and I would beg my mother to bake us this cake. Now I'm just begging her not to sue me for publishing it (her lawyer is a pit bull!). With a little makeover, thanks to prizewinning chef Anna Ginsberg, the recipe is now officially immortal!

Nonstick baking spray with flour
    added (such as Pam for Baking)
¼   cup butter (½ stick), softened
2   tablespoons granulated sugar
⅔   cup chopped pecans
2   tablespoons mini chocolate chips
2¼ cups all-purpose flour
2   teaspoons baking soda
1   teaspoon salt
1   cup butter (2 sticks), softened
½   cup granulated sugar
½   cup packed brown sugar
2   teaspoons vanilla
4   eggs
¾   cup buttermilk
⅓   cup Irish cream liqueur
    (such as Baileys)
1¾ cups mini chocolate pieces
    Chocolate Topping (optional)

1 * Preheat the oven to 350°F. Coat a 12-cup fluted tube pan with the nonstick baking spray.

2 * For the topping, in a small bowl combine the ¼ cup butter and 2 tablespoons granulated sugar until creamy. Stir in the nuts and 2 tablespoons chocolate chips. Spoon into the bottom of the prepared pan; place pan in refrigerator while you make the cake batter.

3 * For the cake, in a bowl stir together the flour, baking soda, and salt. In a large mixing bowl beat the 1 cup butter with an electric mixer until creamy. Add the ½ cup granulated sugar, brown sugar, and vanilla; beat for 1 minute. Add the eggs one at a time, beating for 30 seconds after each addition. Combine the buttermilk and Irish cream. With the mixer on low speed, add the flour and buttermilk mixtures alternately to the batter, mixing well after each addition. Stir in the 1¾ cups chocolate chips. Pour the batter into the prepared pan.

4 * Bake about 50 minutes or until a wooden skewer inserted into the cake comes out clean. Immediately invert the cake onto a cooling rack and let cool completely. If desired, drizzle with Chocolate Topping.

NOTE: For best results, have all ingredients at room temperature.

CHOCOLATE TOPPING: In a small saucepan combine 1 cup mini chocolate chips and 2 teaspoons shortening over low heat. Stir until melted.

HOLY GRAIL OF OPTIONS ∨

BUTTERSCOTCH   CHERRY   MINT CHOCOLATE   PEANUT BUTTER

If chocolate isn't your "thing" (weirdo!), give some of these other chip options a try in this recipe: butterscotch, cherry, peanut butter, mint, or white chocolate chips.

DEEP-FRIED CHEESECAKE NUGGETS

FREEZE: 1 hour / PREP: 10 minutes / COOK: 5 minutes / YIELD: 8 to 10 servings

You'd think that deep-frying one of the richest desserts
in creation would be overkill. You'd be wrong. Enough said.

1 7-inch purchased cheesecake,
    cut into bite-size pieces
   Peanut oil
1 egg
1 tablespoon milk
1 cup panko (Japanese-style
    bread crumbs)
1 teaspoon cinnamon (optional)
   Raspberry Coulis (page 215)
   Purchased chocolate sauce

1 * Freeze cheesecake pieces about 1 hour or until very cold.
In a deep-fat fryer or deep saucepan heat oil to 365°F. In a shallow
bowl beat together egg and milk. In another shallow bowl mix bread
crumbs and, if using, cinnamon. Dip cheesecake into egg mixture,
then roll in bread crumbs.

2 * Fry a few pieces at a time for 20 to 30 seconds or until golden
brown. Serve immediately with Raspberry Coulis and chocolate sauce.

HOLY GRAIL OF OPTIONS ⌄

Peanut oil has a higher
smoking point than most
oils, making it better to
use for high-temperature
cooking and frying.
But you can also
use vegetable oil or
shortening. Avoid butter,
which has a smoking
point of 350°F.

PB&J BREAD CRUST PUDDING

PREP: 20 minutes / BAKE: 45 minutes / YIELD: 8 to 10 servings

You'll feel like a kid again as the unmistakable aroma of PB&J envelops your kitchen. Only now, instead of a squashed sandwich from the hazmat container that doubled as your lunch box, a moist, flavorful, lip-smacking bread pudding delivers the delicious goods.

Butter
4 cups milk
6 eggs, at room temperature
1 cup creamy peanut butter
½ cup sugar
1 tablespoon vanilla
¼ teaspoon salt
8 cups coarsely chopped fresh or day-old white bread or baguette
1 cup desired flavor jelly, jam, or preserves

1* Preheat the oven to 350°F. Lightly butter a 13×9×2-inch baking pan.

2* In a blender combine 2 cups of the milk, the eggs, peanut butter, sugar, vanilla, and salt; blend until smooth, taking care that the peanut butter is thoroughly emulsified into the mixture. Pour into a large bowl; whisk in the remaining 2 cups milk. Stir in the bread and set aside to soak about 10 minutes. Pour into the prepared baking pan. Place spoonfuls of your favorite jelly, jam, or preserves around the bread mixture, pushing them in a bit with your spoon.

3* Bake about 45 minutes or until the pudding is browned, puffed, and a little firm. Let cool. Cut into squares to serve.

HOLY GRAIL OF OPTIONS ∨

SUNFLOWER
HAZELNUT
CASHEW
ALMOND

Peanut butter is king, but any nut butter makes for a tasty variation to this treat.

DULCE DE LECHE TRIFLE

PREP: 12 minutes / YIELD: 12 servings

Soaked in the sweet, silky goodness that is dulce de leche, this trifle shouldn't be trifled with. It should, however, be eaten. And, of course, shared. Dulce de leche can be found at most international supermarkets, but you can also make your own.

4 cups strawberries, sliced
2 bananas, sliced
6 biscotti, crushed
1 purchased angel food cake, crumbled
1 (24-ounce) container frozen whipped dessert topping, thawed
1 (13.4-ounce) can dulce de leche
1 (8-ounce) bottle chocolate sauce

1 * In a large trifle bowl or 12 dessert dishes layer the strawberries, bananas, biscotti, cake, and dessert topping, drizzling the dulce de leche and chocolate sauce between layers and saving a generous portion of each for the top.

TO MAKE DULCE DE LECHE: Pour one 14-ounce can sweetened condensed milk into the top of a double boiler; cover and place over boiling water. Cook over low heat, stirring occasionally, for 60 to 75 minutes or until thick and a light caramel color. Remove from heat. Beat with an electric mixer until smooth.

SO THAT'S HOW YOU DO IT ⌄

Making dulce de Leche with sweetened condensed milk is a piece of cake. Just follow the directions above.

TWINKIE TIRAMISU

PREP: 15 minutes / CHILL: 2 hours / YIELD: 6 to 8 servings

My version of this recipe omits sugar in the brewed coffee to balance out the sweetness of the Twinkies (yeah, they're kind of sweet, it turns out). I do believe you'll find the results tiramisuperb and twinkilicious.

8   cream-filled sponge cakes
     (recommended: Twinkies)
1   cup unsweetened brewed
     espresso or strong coffee
1½ cups whipping cream
⅓   cup sugar
2   (8.75-ounce) packages mascarpone
     cheese, at room temperature
10 vanilla wafer cookies, crushed, or
     5 vanilla wafer cookies, crushed and
     5 chocolate wafer cookies, crushed
     (optional)

1* Cut the sponge cakes in half lengthwise and fit the bottom halves into an 11×7×1½-inch pan. Drizzle with ½ cup of the coffee.

2* Whip the cream and sugar to soft peaks. In a large bowl whisk the mascarpone a bit to loosen it; fold in the whipped cream. Pour half of the mixture over the sponge cakes and spread evenly. Make another layer with the tops of the sponge cakes; drizzle with the remaining coffee. Spread mascarpone mixture evenly over the sponge cakes.

3* Sprinkle crushed vanilla wafer cookies over mascarpone mixture. Or, if desired, gently place several different-size round cookie cutters on the surface of the mascarpone mixture. Carefully sprinkle the crushed vanilla wafers into a few of the cookie cutters and the crushed chocolate wafers into the remaining cutters. Gently remove cookie cutters. Lightly cover and refrigerate at least 2 hours before serving.

GEORGE'S SECRET ⌄

If your local grocer doesn't carry mascarpone cheese, make your own with half ricotta cheese and half whipped cream cheese.

RASPBERRY AND AVOCADO TRIFLE

PREP: 15 minutes / CHILL: 1 hour / YIELD: 8 servings

In Brazil avocados are used strictly for desserts. So one night (after a couple-few Caipirinhas), I decided to try them in that quintessentially British delight, the trifle! Turns out that sweetened avocados bring a smooth richness tailor-made for this decadent dessert.

4   ripe avocados, halved and pitted
2   tablespoons fresh lime juice
⅔   cup sugar
1   cup fresh raspberries (reserve
        8 for garnish)
½   cup unsweetened coconut milk
2   cups crumbled angel food cake
        (about half of a purchased cake)
½   cup roasted pistachio nuts,
        coarsely chopped
      Fresh raspberries
      Avocado slices
      Pistachios

1 * Scoop the avocado flesh into a medium bowl. Mash with the lime juice and ⅓ cup of the sugar until smooth. In another bowl mash the raspberries with the remaining ⅓ cup sugar and the coconut milk.

2 * Put some crumbled angel food cake in the bottom of 8 champagne flutes or wineglasses. In each glass, layer the avocado mixture, some pistachios, and some raspberry-coconut mixture. Repeat the layers. Garnish each glass with a raspberry, an avocado slice, and some pistachios. Chill at least 1 hour before serving.

MYSTERY THINGAMAJIGS ⌄

Our long national avocado-peeling nightmare is over, thanks to this nifty little gadget!

PIÑA COLADA CRISP

PREP: 10 minutes / BAKE: 45 minutes / COOL: 10 minutes / YIELD: 8 to 10 servings

When I'm having a tough day and want to escape my troubles, I'm like a lot of people: I just picture myself on a tropical island . . . in a lounge chair . . . waves lapping at my feet . . . munching on this delicious coconutty treat.

1	tablespoon butter
1	(20-ounce) can pineapple chunks, drained
6	cups coarse bread crumbs
¾	cup powdered sugar
½	cup unsweetened coconut milk
1	cup flaked coconut
¾	cup pecans, chopped
3	tablespoons granulated sugar
½	cup butter (1 stick), melted
	Vanilla ice cream or frozen yogurt
	Toasted flaked coconut (optional)

1 * Preheat the oven to 375°F. Grease an 8-inch round cake pan with the 1 tablespoon butter.

2 * In a bowl mix the pineapple chunks with 4 cups of the bread crumbs, the powdered sugar, and coconut milk. In another bowl mix the remaining 2 cups bread crumbs and the 1 cup coconut, pecans, granulated sugar, and melted butter. Place the pineapple mixture in the prepared pan; top with the coconut mixture.

3 * Bake for 45 minutes or until browned. Cool for 10 minutes before serving. Scoop crisp into bowls and top with vanilla ice cream. If desired, sprinkle with toasted coconut.

Useless Facts: Oid you know that the piña colada is the official drink of Puerto Rico? I'll drink to that!

DURAN'S RULES FOR GASTRONOMIC GLEE

With more than 6,569 entries and counting, my ever-growing guide to culinary convention will hopefully be available soon in an attractive set of four ostrich-skin bound volumes (with bonus "a version" featuring Cate Blanchett in the role of George Duran available for download). Until then culled for you a random selection as an *amuse-bouche*. **BON APPÉTIT!**

#08 WHEN IT COMES TO STEAK, THERE REALLY SHOULD BE A TERM FOR BETWEEN RARE AND RAW.

#25 BROCCOLI IS A GREAT SOURCE OF VITAMIN C... BUT A TERRIBLE BASIS FOR A MILK SHAKE.

#78 THERE IS NO SUCH THING AS TOO MUCH PEPPERONI.

#89 IF YOU'RE EATING A HOT DOG MADE FROM TOFU, YOU, MY FRIEND, ARE NOT EATING A HOT DOG.

#235 PEOPLE WHO HATE FOIE GRAS ARE SOME OF MY FAVORITE PEOPLE. MORE FOR ME.

#447 ANYONE WHO USES A KNIFE AND A FORK TO EAT RIBS FOREVER LOSES THE RIGHT TO EAT RIBS.

#515 IF YOU'RE SERVED A CHICKEN BREAST THAT IS LARGER THAN A HUMAN HEAD, RUN.

#991 LETTUCE AND TOMATO IN A HAMBURGER DO NOT QUALIFY AS A SALAD. NOW, ADD A COUPLE SLICES OF RADISH AND CUCUMBER AND I MIGHT LET YOU SLIDE.

#1,800 WHEN COUGHING AT THE TABLE, ALWAYS FLASH THE "I'M COUGHING, NOT CHOKING" SYMBOL TO WARD OFF OVERZEALOUS HEIMLICH MANEUVER-ERS!